50P.

CW00872230

WILD MUSHROOMS

WILD MUSHROOMS

An Illustrated Handbook
by
LINUS ZEITLMAYR

Translated and Adapted from the German,
with Mushroom Recipes
by
Otto Gregory

With Illustrations by
Claus Caspari

FREDERICK MULLER

This book was first published in Germany by the Droemersche Verlagsanstalt
T. Knaur Nachf, in 1955 under the title KNAURS PILZBUCH. The present
translation (from the latest, 1965, edition) is slightly abridged

First published in Great Britain 1968

by Frederick Muller Ltd., London, NW2 6LE

Copyright © 1955 by Th. Knaur Nachf. Verlag, München
English translation Copyright © Frederick Muller Ltd.

ISBN 0 584 10324 7

Printed and bound in Great Britain by The Garden City Press Limited
Letchworth, Hertfordshire SG6 1JS

Reprinted 1976

CONTENTS

TRANSLATOR'S FOREWORD

"People of British stock are quite content to dismiss mycophobia as a social phenomenon hardly worth discussing. 'After all', they say, 'most mushrooms are poisonous, so why not play safe? There are plenty of other things to eat. Why grub around under rotten tree stumps for nasty-looking fungi? Leave that to the Slavs. Life is cheap behind the Iron Curtain!' Yet only three ★ European mushrooms, *Amanita phalloides* and two others, which experts alone can differentiate from it, are in fact lethal. You might as well refuse raspberries because the deadly nightshade is poisonous; or apples because of the terrible manchineel."

Robert Graves

Some 28,000 tons of cultivated mushrooms are consumed annually in Britain and no less than 55,000 tons of the same cultivated variety are used each year in the United States. So there is no doubt that the flavour of mushrooms is well liked and that the mutual mycophobia – fear of fungi – traditional to both countries, is confined to the wild varieties. Yet all who know the wild variety of the common mushroom agree that its flavour is incomparably finer, more tasty, than that of its cultivated cousin. A number of the other wild fungi are equally good to eat.

Those who have been on the Continent in the late Summer or Autumn may have eaten and enjoyed a dish of one or other of the local wild fungi. They will agree that these also have a fine and savoury flavour but, even to-day, few people realise that these same wild fungi which they have met in Continental restaurants grow plentifully in our English woods, or on our heaths and pastures and are as fine and savoury to eat here as they are in France or Germany, Italy or Austria.

For those who do know that they grow here there is the problem of where to look, and of knowing which are good to eat, which poisonous. There are, after all, at least 3,000 different species of larger fungi in Britain alone. (Among these there are only four deadly-poisonous species, with another five which may be dangerous and are better left alone.)

★ To-day a fourth species, *Inocybe patouillardii* must be included among the lethal species.

This book by a leading German expert on fungi should help to make them more popular over here. The author worked for many years at the Fungi Advisory Centre in Munich, helping beginners to distinguish the good species from the dangerous ones and his book is written to do just that. The book includes all the best of the edible species, any dangerous species with which these might be confused, and the few poisonous ones.

What has helped to make this book exceedingly popular on the Continent are the brilliant colour illustrations by the leading German artist in Natural History. In these days of perfect colour photography, it might be thought that colour photos would be the ideal way to illustrate a book on fungi. But the camera cannot select and emphasize sufficiently, and the characteristics which may distinguish a particular species are often too subtle for the camera. In these portraits of fungi, the artist–who, like the author, knows and loves fungi–has shown every species in its most revealing pose, making identification very much easier. Indeed, where useful he gives several portraits of the same fungus. In the case of the deadly *Inocybe patouillardii* for instance, which it is essential to know well, he gives no less than five pictures of the same fungus in various stages of development.

Newcomers to fungi will want to know whether all the species described actually grow in Britain. The answer is that, with a few exceptions due to soil and climate, fungi are universal throughout Europe, and indeed much further afield. All the species described in this book occur in Britain, and many of them also occur in North America and elsewhere.

Beginners, confronted with seventy different species, many of them superficially similar, may be confused. To these I suggest beginning with just six species, all of them edible and good to eat, all fairly common in season, all easily recognised and none, provided descriptions and illustrations are studied likely to be confused with any dangerous species.

The six, with the numbers of their descriptions, are:

The Shaggy Cap or Lawyer's Wig (27)
The Wood Blewit (11)
The Cep, *(Boletus edulis)* (46)
The Chanterelle (44)
The Parasol Mushroom (8)
The Saffron Milk Cap, *(Lactarius deliciosus)* (30)

Study the pictures and the descriptions of these six, and the characteristics of the few poisonous species (none of which resembles any of these) and you will be equipped to begin your first 'fungus foray'. Here it may be mentioned, for those who wish to search for fungi in the company of more experienced enthusiasts, that The British Mycological Society holds a number of fungus forays each year at which students and visitors are welcome. (Address: R. L. Lucas Esq., Hon. Sec., The British Mycological Society, Department of Agriculture, University of Oxford.)

But if you are alone: where to look? Depending on the prediliction of the various species for particular trees (detailed in the descriptions) it is worth looking for fungi, in season, in any wood or even around isolated trees while, for grassland fungi, open downs or any area of pasture are worth searching. However, the best of all woods for fungi are areas of ancient forest. The New Forest, perhaps on account of its climate, is especially rich in fungi. Burnham Beeches in Buckinghamshire also has a good reputation and any similar areas of ancient forest are worth searching.

There is no golden rule to distinguish edible and poisonous species and so the only rule is to be absolutely sure of what you are collecting and proposing to eat. It is wise, before collecting anything to eat, to study and learn the characteristics of the few dangerous, deadly-poisonous species.

To identify a fungus, check it against the illustration which you think resembles it and then check the various characteristics against the description. For identification the important points are: colour and shape of cap, gills or tubes, attachment of gills or tubes to stem, presence or absence of ring and/or volva, smell and taste, colour of spores (the spores are not necessarily the same colour as the gills and it may be necessary to make a spore-print, p. 21-22). Finally, but this applies only to advanced workers who wish to identify some rare species, the size of the spores is measured under a microscope. It should be mentioned here that special care is needed with young fungi with unopened caps since these can be difficult to identify.

In preparing this English edition English names have been used for the species when genuine English names exist. In cases where the botanical (Latin) name has been revised, the revised generic or specific names are used, with the earlier name in brackets where this is considered useful. For travellers who may find themselves abroad in the fungus season, French, Italian, German and (occasionally) Spanish names are given for those edible species which may be encountered in restaurants. Since the various species sometimes appear on foreign menus under the generic title 'fungi', it may also be useful to give some common foreign names: Fr., *Champignons,* It., *Funghi,* German, *Pilze,* Austrian, *Schwämmerl,* Spanish, *Setas.*

In this English edition a selection of Fungus Recipes is included, and also an English Bibliography.

My thanks are due to Mr. T. N. Parkin who has read this entire manuscript, has made a great many helpful suggestions and has given valuable and unstinting assistance throughout the preparation of this translation, and, for the culinary section, to Mrs. Lyne who, by example in her own home has for long stimulated my appreciation of elegant cuisine.

Otto Gregory

AUTHOR'S FOREWORD TO THE GERMAN EDITION

Another mushroom-fungus book? Any fairly expert, amateur fungus hunter is bound to ask this question after an anxious look at the, by-no-means short row of fungus books already on his shelves.

Nevertheless–here *is* another one! Because–and only because–this new one hopes to win over, and to enthuse, new amateur fungus friends, and by presenting the whole thing in a new way, perhaps encourage them sufficiently to start them studying seriously.

Even the author himself wondered for a long time whether he ought to add one of his own to the excellent descriptions of our native edible and inedible fungi which already exist. However, any number of people, no less expert, said 'Yes' with such emphasis that I was encouraged to begin. Then, there was so much enthusiasm and so many requests from members of the Bavarian Botanical Society that all my doubts vanished. I am not exactly a newcomer to the subject and its problems and I am not really without some knowledge of what is wanted. This came to me easily as a result of practical work at the Fungi Advisory Centre and also as a result of enormous numbers of questions put to me on fungus forays. On the whole, the existing books failed to provide the answers. I was myself able to gain some insight into what was wanted largely as a result of the training I received from those two grand-old-men of practical and theoretical mycology, both from Munich, Professor Michael Merkl and Florian Lorenz and I would like to repay my gratitude to these two deeply honoured friends by dedicating to them my little book as public appreciation of their own, quite unrewarded, but wonderfully fruit-ful, influence.

My final doubts were removed by my friend Claus Caspari, whose already well-known work–taking from Nature those brilliancies which only a scientifically-minded artist knows how to see and so, how to record–had already achieved such splendid success. Now he was anxious to collaborate with me on a fungus book.

So perhaps this book is more than just one more traditional guide to fungi because it really does say more about the lives and secrets of this strange group of plants than is usually to be found in fungus books. However, the best possible help towards understanding them are the really masterly portraits of the fungi which Claus Caspari has created.

Intended for the general reader, it may be said that this book is limited to essentials and, as a pocket book, that it can only present a selection from these. Yet–however distant the goal which every nature lover strives to reach–how wonderful the path towards it!

As the basis for my book I used the 'Mushroom-Toadstool' book of my boyhood; that old, 1905 book by Sydow, which I must thank for my first insight into the world of fungi. Yet even on this basis I have been obliged to cut down. I did not intend this to be a definitive work; partly because I know from experience that definitive treatises are not usually much good to beginners, and partly for reasons of space to which any would-be pocket book must submit. Serious fungus lovers who want to know the subject more scientifically should consult the bibliography which they will find at the end of this book. It is certainly no criticism of Meinhard Moser's book that only an advanced fungus lover can use it really successfully. Those who want to identify with complete certainty will have to refer to his book, the more so, since none of the earlier books can replace it from the point of view of nomenclature. The very latest, from another linguistic sphere, and dealing with questions of systematic classification, the 'Flore Anylitique des Champignons Supérieurs' by Kuhner and Romagnesi (Paris 1953) seems, for that very reason, at present to concern only experts.

Finally, my warm thanks to Dr. Werner Botticher for friendly advice and active support.

Linus Zeitlmayr

WHAT ARE FUNGI?

The green plants, enormous in number and in variety of forms, colours, and scents obtain what they need from the air and sunlight. Minute green particles, millions in every leaf, are the machinery of their existence. These grains of chlorophyl, (chlorophyll simply means 'leaf-green'), catch the energy inherent in sunlight. Using this, the plant achieves the commonplace, yet ever new, miracle: it transforms inanimate matter—water, salts, and the carbon dioxide in the atmosphere—into the components of living things—carbohydrates, fats, proteins—and, greatest miracle of all, changes these into actual living organisms.

So green plants were the earliest form of visible life among dead matter. Animal life can only exist if there are green plants to provide it with initial nourishment. For all living organisms (human beings included), which feed as animals, owe their existence directly or indirectly to the green chlorophyll in plants.

However, not all plants are green. Some plants, lacking chlorophyll, cannot themselves build up the substances they need for existence. So, in the same way as animals, these have to take what they need for their own existence from other living things. They become parasites, sucking life from extraneous organisms, which perish as a result, and killing in order to survive themselves. Yet not all plants without chlorophyll are parasites which only survive at the expense of other lives. Countless organisms are satisfied with what some other living thing discards and so create a new form of life from dead and decaying matter. Among these are the fungi.

The lives and activities of the fungi seem strange to us and, in the changes they undergo, uncanny. Ancient legends and fairy tales credit these tiny plants with tremendous powers to affect us for good or evil. However, they keep to their own peaceful realm into which we cannot intrude to disturb their harmony.

To most people the word fungi means mushrooms and toadstools. These are the relatively large, often brightly-coloured, capped fungi to be found in woods and meadows. But the moulds which cover decaying fruit, carelessly-stored bread, or remnants of food or liquid which have been kept too long are also fungi. We have hardly any conception of the curious forms these fungi take, and we know most of them only by hearsay, seldom from our own observation. Occasionally we do hear of yeast fungus, or we may use bakers' or brewers' yeast, or we may know of moulds in wine and beer, but the average man has no conception of the thousands of shapes and different modes of life of all those fungi which he cannot see. After all, few people keep a powerful magnifying glass or a microscope in general use at home, and few bother about the invisible life which goes on all around. We owe it to research workers, using magnifying glasses and microscopes in their daily work, that an entire world of minute and invisible organisms has been opened up. Countless living organisms belong to it: the single-cell animals and plants, and the bacteria. They are all microscopically small; that is, never visible to the naked eye, and the most important fungi are among them. But the average man has no conception of this when he comes across mushrooms or the variously-coloured fungi in the fields and woods.

FOLKLORE AND LEGEND

There are many fairy tales and folk songs about fungi–'The little people of the woods'. Ancient legends tell stories of strange beings with fat bellies and round hats appearing suddenly in the woods and then, always cloaked in secrecy and magic, suddenly vanishing.

From this ancient consciousness of magic some vestiges still live on in popular superstition. In parts of Bavaria and Austria, for instance, the appearance of mushrooms and toadstools is believed to depend on the gods of Nature. The belief probably goes back to the ancient gods, Donar and Wotan, and was later transferred to their Christian counterparts, that is to God and his Saints: St. Peter, patron of the weather; St. Vitus, descendant of the Slav sun-god, Svantevit; and to St. Procopius and St. Anthony the Hermit.

Or else devils, witches, elves, and good and evil spirits are thought to be responsible for the growth of fungi and little offerings or 'mushroom prayers' are made to all of these.

The Fly Agaric *(Amanita muscaria)*, thought to be one of the most poisonous fungi, and also the puff-balls are 'Devil's Work', 'Devil's Bread', or 'Devil's Snuff'. 'It rains mushrooms and toadstools' on St. Peter and St. Paul's Day is another legend. St. Peter, the Bavarian *'Donnerpeter'*, whose anniversary is 29th July is said to sow 'fungus seeds'. On St. Peter's and St. Paul's day it is believed 'to rain mushrooms'. St. Veit, on his anniversary, 15th June, is supposed to ride at night through the woods on a blind, white horse–as did Wotan once –sowing mushroom seeds. On St. Procopius' day (4th July) it also 'rains mushrooms'. St. Anthony the Great, the Hermit, whose symbol, a pig, has mythological connections with fungi, patron saint of swineherds and swine merchants, is also patron of fungus collectors and dealers in fungi. As a hermit, he wanders through the forests with his staff, on which there is a bell, dispersing the evil spirits which hide the good mushrooms from human view.

Then there are beliefs about 'betraying mushrooms', that is certain fungi which reveal or betray the presence of the edible Ceps, the *Boletus edulis*. Among these are the *Amanita muscaria,* the *Lactarius piperatus,* and the *Boletus scaber,* as well as varieties of the Common Mushroom.

Experienced fungus gatherers will know that there is a grain of truth in this legend.

Some species of fungi grow in circles, forming the so-called 'fairy rings', and these have given rise to various popular superstitions. According to one of these, the more luxurient growth of grass, or its sparseness, is the scene of the nightly dances or festivals of the 'mushroom fairies', elves, and spirits.

To-day there are various scientific explanations of this phenomenon which will be discussed later.

FUNGI IN HISTORY

We can only guess how ancient and prehistoric men learned to distinguish wholesome foods from dangerous and poisonous ones. Before they discovered which of the fungi they found everywhere in woods and meadows were harmless, countless lives must have been lost as a result of eating the poisonous varieties. No historical record tells us anything about this or about the beginning of human culture. Indications that prehistoric peoples ate or used fungi are rare, though O. Heer (1866) and others have found traces of puff-balls and other fungi in stone-age dwellings in Switzerland, Württemberg and Austria which may have been used as tinder to light fires.

In ancient India, Egypt, and Babylonia, and then, in classical times, among the Greeks and Romans, poisonous fungi were known as well as several, much sought-after, edible varieties. It is only from classical times that various names for fungi have been handed down to us: 'Bolites, Agarikon, Amanita'. Theophrastos of Eresos on Lesbos about 312 or 320 B.C., the Greek naturalist and pupil of Aristotle, mentions fungi ('mykes'), truffles? ('hydnon'), puff-balls? ('pezis') and Dung-fungi. Nicander (150 B.C.) writes of fungus poisoning and the Roman poet, Horace (born 65 B.C.), in one of his satires, praises 'pratenses', presumably field mushrooms, as the best of the fungi. Cornelius Celsus, a writer on medical matters about 38 B.C., mentions strange remedies for fungus poisoning. Dioscorides, the Greek doctor and writer on Natural History, about 60 B.C., describes Truffles, praises them as good to eat, and mentions the cultivation of fungi as well as poisonous fungi. The Roman naturalist, Pliny the Elder, who died in 79 A.D. exploring Vesuvius, devotes more than one chapter of his Natural History to fungi. He deals in detail with Truffles, describes the Amanita caesaria and the Boletus edulis as delicacies and also their preparation–which the masters did not leave to their slaves but carried out themselves, using costly cutlery of amber and expensive silver utensils.

Pliny recalls frequent deaths among the families of Roman consuls due to fungi. He knows Tinder-fungi, Puff-balls, the Fomes fomentarius, and other woodland fungi. The ancient Romans were as sophisticated in the pleasures of the table as they were in the fine arts and the luxurious and extravagent feasts of Lucullus have become deservedly proverbial. So there are likely to have been not-infrequant cases of fungus poisoning, by accident or design. One (unconfirmed) legend claims that Euripides, the Athenian poet, lost in one day his wife, daughter, and two sons through fungus poisoning.

According to Pliny, the Roman Emperor Claudius was poisoned in 54 A.D. by his wife Agrippina with a dish of fungi. A little later, Nero's Prefect of the Guard, Serenus, a friend of Seneca, with several other officers of the Imperial Guard also lost their lives as a result of fungi.

Pliny also describes how fungi can cure certain illnesses and Martial, famous for his epigrams, in one of them, praises his host, who was as gluttonous as he was mean, for the *Amanita caesarea* he was offered, and grumbles about the *Boletus luridas*.

Suetonius, (75-160 A.D.), historian of the Imperial times, recounts the generosity of Tiberius towards the poet Sabinus for a prize poem in fable form in honour of the *Amanita caesarea*. The famous physician, Galen (born 131 A.D., died at the beginning of the 3rd century) praises the *Amanita caesarea* and the Champignon as the best of the fungi and recommends chicken droppings as a remedy for fungus poisoning. (Can this suggestion by the celebrated physician perhaps be a premonition of the very latest therapy using Moulds and Ray Fungi?).

Much later, Paracelsus, who died in 1541, prescribed something not very different–perhaps because of the ancient tradition as well as for valid reasons.

Athenaeus, Greek Sophist and Grammarian about 228, knew that Champignons could be dried and writes, almost in a modern manner, about fungus cultivation.

Cassanius Bassius of Bythynia, who published by command of the Byzantine Emperor Constantine VII, an encyclopaedia–the twenty books of the Geoponica–with extracts from numerous works by ancient agricultural writers, is more detailed and describes a method of cultivating fungi reminiscent of modern experiments in growing fungi on tree trunks and branches.

As far as we know to-day, the Middle Ages did little to enlarge the knowledge of the Ancients on Botany, and therefore on fungi. There was little personal observation and, apart from the Church, un-conditional belief in tradition was the absolute rule. Bishop Thietmar of Merseburg reports in his Chronicle of the year 1018 a case of serious fungus poisoning of which seven journeymen were the victims. St. Hildegard of Bingen (died 1180), the first researcher into Natural History and a versatile doctor, has little new to say about mycology and the little she adds is cloudy and uncertain. Nevertheless, she does know several fungi, both from the point of view of edibility as well as for their medicinal properties: among others the *Elaphomyces* and various Tree Fungi, as well as the *Merulius lacrimans,* all too well-known to-day as 'Dry Rot'.

The Dominican monk and Bishop of Regensburg, Albertus Magnus, who died a hundred years after St. Hildegard, brilliant as he was in other directions, kept entirely to tradition as far as mycology was concerned and simply copied Dioscorides. As a doctor, Albertus Magnus gives the first medical description of a case of fungus poisoning. In his work 'De Vegetabilibus libri septem' he does mention fungi and distinguishes clearly between them and other plants, but he is not yet clear about their nature. He knows certain 'little round mushrooms which appear in the Spring and disappear in May', but whether he is referring to Agarics, the St. George's Mushroom, or to Morels it is impossible to know. He also describes certain features as indicating that a fungus is poisonous; mentioning a sticky, or clammy, moist cap, and colour changes after picking, and he refers to the Fly Agaric as poisonous. He also knows Truffles and how to prepare them, but he does not think much of them, or of fungi in general.

Konrad of Megenberg, a Canon of Regensburg about 1350, the first German writer on Natural History, refers to the Spring mushrooms of Albertus Magnus, probably correctly, as Morels.

The Middle Ages ends, from the point of view of Natural History and Mycology, with the 'Fathers of Botany', those authors of the magnificent 16th century Herbals: Bock, Matthiolus and Clusius. These scholars were already close to the present day in their approach, showed independent observation, and began to test and experiment seriously.

Among historical personages who died of fungus poisoning are: Buddha (about 480 B.C. in India); the Emperor Diocletian (unconfirmed), 313 A.D.; Pope Clement VII, 1534; the Emperor Karl VII, 1740, as well as the patron of Mozart, Jean Schobert, with his wife, child, and three friends.

MYCOLOGY

ORIGIN-AGE-AND NUMBER OF FUNGI

The mushrooms and toadstools which we know are not the actual fungus plants. The plants themselves are barely visible, or quite invisible, to the naked eye and their life-history was not revealed until the coming of the microscope. Modern microscopy entails a highly-developed and thoroughly complicated technique involving the dyeing and mounting of specimens and biological training is essential. However, any exact knowledge of the larger fungi is impossible without an understanding of their anatomy and of their development from the original cell to the complicated structures of the large fruit bodies. All attempts at a logical classification must stem from this.

The science of mycology is a branch of botany. In 1735 the father of botany as we now understand it, the famous Swedish botanist Linnaeus, divided the vegetable kingdom into two great classes. Plants with clearly visible reproductive organs he called Phanerogams (= flowering plants). Those without clearly visible sex organs he called Cryptogams (= hidden flowering).

To-day the vegetable kingdom is divided in accordance with a natural system into four divisions:

1. Thallophyta ⎫
2. Bryophyta ⎬ Spore-bearing plants or Cryptogams
3. Pteridophyta ⎭
4. Spermatophyta } Seed-bearing plants or Phanerogams

these divisions being classified, as indicated, into spore bearing plants and seed bearing plants.

It is difficult to describe the essentials of fungi in simple words. What is formulated so concisely in scientific language can here only be made clear by describing their structure and life cycles.

The true fungi are those Thallophytae (with cell-nuclei and without chlorophyll) which have adopted a parasitic or saprophytic way of life. We do not include among these the bacteria or the slime-fungi (myxomycetes). Only in the simplest group, the Archemycetes, is the body of the fungus naked. Otherwise the cells are surrounded by a transparent-hyalin-membrane. The cell walls of the larger fungi consist of chitin-a material otherwise only found in the animal world as the outer covering of insects, spiders, and similar creatures. Genuine cellulose, which forms the cell walls of other plants, is not present in fungi. Their cells, in common with those of all living things, whether animal or vegetable, are composed-in addition to fats and starches-of the mysterious substance, protoplasm. Clorophyll, which is otherwise present in all plants, is absent from all fungi, although these do have many types of colouring matter as well as resins, minerals, and odour producing substances. Chemical investigation of the higher fungi is still in its infancy although to some extent advanced with the lower fungi.

Fungi are a group of organisms of very varied origins. Because they decompose so rapidly, fossilized fungi from earlier geological periods have only been preserved in especially favourable circumstances. The earliest of these are from the mid-Devonian period—that is from the middle-period of the earth's history—more than 300 million years ago. Living in humus, as so-called saprophytes and parasites, they naturally depended on the existence of land plants since, without chlorophyll, they could only exist on other living organisms or on their remains. So their earliest forms can only be deduced from those of to-day. Fungi probably originated from water-algae (flagellates) and tube-algae (siphonales) which, after gradually losing their chlorophyll, were no longer able to exist independently. As a result of this different mode of living they branched away from their ancestors and so were obliged to find a new means of existence suited to life on land. The sex organs retrogressed, the process of fertilization was split chronologically and spacially into conception (plasmogamy—the approach of the nuclei) and the nuclear union (karyogamy), and further development to the present forms which we know know as fungi followed.

The total number of all types of fungus known to-day amounts to about 100,000. They live in all geographical situations and conditions of climate from the equator to both poles, but have only been fairly extensively studied in Europe and the U.S.A.

Those which we gather to eat, or recognize as poisonous, or admire as delightful, if apparently useless, ornaments of the woods belong mostly to the larger cap fungi and puff balls, that is, to the more easily numbered giants among the fungi. Even so, these represent quite a considerable number—in Great Britain alone, some 3,000 species.

THE MYCELIUM

The fungi which we see growing in the woods and meadows are merely the fruit-bodies of the plant which is itself so sensitive that it would quickly die if exposed to the air and light. The actual fungus plant lives underground and it is the reproductive organ which is sent above ground to develop. (Fig. 1)

If we dig up a fungus carefully we find an extensive, wide-spreading web of white strands of fibres with growing tips. These look like fine roots but they are, in fact, the essential plant, the thallophyte. The thallophyte lives in the ground on decomposed animal and vegetable matter and, in cooperation with countless soil algae and tiny animal organisms, plays an essential part in maintaining the fertility of the soil.

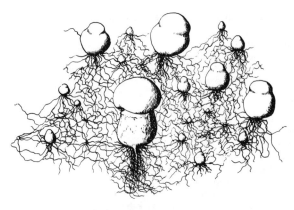

Fig. 1: Mycelium with fruit bodies and young fungi

We have already said that the green plants contain a dye–chlorophyll–which has remarkable properties. By means of this, with the help of light-energy on water and carbon dioxide in the air they can nourish themselves. Fungi, on the other hand, have no such colouring matter and are not self-supporting in their nourishment. So they are always dependent on pre-formed nutrient matter, living on decayed matter which they decompose in obtaining their own nourishment.

Such organisms, which cause decomposition and which make use of decomposed matter, are called Saprophytes. Living beside them in enormous numbers are minute, similarly-shaped fungi–mostly only recognisable under the microscope–known as Parasites because, instead of living on dead matter, these nourish themselves on living plants and even on living animals. Because they are so small they have not been known for long and they are now recognised as often causing plant or animal diseases. The larger fungi may also live either as saprophytes or as parasites.

Common to all fungi are the threadlike strands (either single- or multi-cellular) known as *hyphae,* the total mass of hyphae together forming the fungus 'spawn' or *mycelium.* The mycelium is the organ of nourishment while the fruit-body, which we call the mushroom or toadstool, is the organ of reproduction. The thin, colourless threads are the first part of the fungus to develop and, as organs of nourishment, they are on, or just under, the surface of the ground. They grow outwards, the outer threads continually growing and branching in every direction, wherever suitable organic nourishment is found, and so they cover an enormous area of ground. The parasites, which grow only on living plants, send out short branches to enable them to cling to the living cells of their host. If they grow on the surface of the host they are known as Epiphytes. If they penetrate into the tissue of the host, sending their threads between the cells, they are called Endophytes.

The area covered by, and the length of life of the mycelium are extremely varied. Some are quite short-lived and will grow on a pine-cone, or a leaf, or even on an old pine-needle; others spread over many square yards of ground in wood or meadow, or grow on large trees, and may go on living for years, if not for centuries. Some forms can live under water, others in darkness and with little air, in cellars or underground passages. Sometimes a number of adjoining threads of mycelium can join together to form thick strands or *rhizomorphs,* and many species of fungi, including the notorious Dry Rot, can live in this form in the ground under decomposing matter, or under the bark or the roots of fallen or diseased trees. Rhizomorphs–meaning root-like–are so called because of their striking similarity with the roots of seed plants. They may form cylindrical or ribbon-like strands several yards long with a firm, dark-brown outer skin and a white core. These are the sterile form of mycelium which can remain dorm-ant for years and, under the right conditions, resume their destructive activity. Among these are the hard, hornlike, bulbous masses of dorm-ant mycelium, rich in nutrient matter, known as *Sclerotium.* A con-siderable number of species can exist in this form.

Often strands of mycelium will unite with the roots of plants in a way which at first seems to be parasitical. However, research has shown that this combination between the roots and the fungus is the reverse and is, in fact, a mutually beneficial relationship between a higher and a lower plant form. Often the mycelium strands do not merely surround the roots of trees or woodland plants but actually penetrate them so that the sap of tree and fungus are mixed. In this way they help each other and it can happen that the lives of the two organisms depend on each other. This mutually beneficial association is known as *Symbiosis* (living together), and the symbiosis of a tree or a plant with a fungus is called *Mycorrhiza.*

Research has shown that this mutually dependent form of living is common to the more important woodland trees, while fungus col-lectors know from their own experience that their favourite fungi are usually found either under certain trees, or at least within the range of its roots. Similarly, it only became possible to grow certain tropical orchids in hot houses when the significance of their root-fungi had been realised.

Certain fungi live in symbiosis with algae, which are thallophytae containing chlorophyll. The union of algae and fungi is especially in-teresting because it produces what, to the casual observer, seems to be a separate species–the universally-distributed Lichens. These are tiny, branched, or leaflike, often beautifully-coloured, plant formations which are found on trees, rocks, or on the ground. Lichens represent something more than an ordinary plant organism. In them, the fungus mycelium and the threads of the algae have come to form a complete unit and have developed such a rich variety of types that they were, for a long time, considered to be a separate branch of the plant kingdom. In this union the algae, with their chlorophyll, provide organic nutrient matter and the fungus provides water, oxides, mineral salts and also, probably, certain hormones. The study of lichens is a specialised and comprehensive branch of mycology and requires special study in addition to botanical knowledge.

Investigation into the life-history of fungus mycelium has also solved the secret of 'Fairy Rings'–the, sometimes large, circles of fungi which have given rise to many legends and nursery stories. It was at first thought that the rings were caused by cattle wandering in circles, and that their manure caused grass, and also fungi to flourish, but it was then found that rings appeared in places where no cattle had been. Finally Kinzel and other researchers discovered that, on suitable soil, the mycelium grows outwards from a central point. Fruit bodies are only formed at the outer extremities and these then appear as a Fairy Ring. The extremities continue to grow while the older parts die off, and so the ring becomes larger year by year.

At these rings, areas of especially luxuriant plant growth occur simultaneously with areas which are completely dead. As a result of observing that, within these rings, the dead grass had not rotted or decayed as it does elsewhere when it dies, the Frenchman, Charles Hollande, discovered that the fungi which cause Fairy Rings, especially species of *Clytocybe,* are able to kill seeds. Rotting and decay is always due to minute organisms, especially to bacteria. If, therefore, the dead grass within the ring does not decay, the fungus growing underneath must release an active substance which destroys or hinders the bacteria. This substance was isolated. It showed anti-bacterial properties similar to Penicillin, which will be discussed later (p. 57). Attempts have been made to utilise this Clitocybin to combat tubercular bacillae.

THE FRUIT-BODY

When the hyphae–the threads of mycelium–have branched and branched again, forming a thick mass which is the fungus flesh, composed of ground-hyphae, growth-hyphae and nutrient-hyphae, they grow upwards parallel to each other, finally breaking through the sub-stratum in which the mycelium has grown, and the surface of the ground, and spread outwards like a fountain (Fig. 2, p. 16). At this stage the stem and cap of the future fruit-body are developed and have the familiar mushroom shape.

This has the task of ensuring the reproduction and the distribution of the fungus and it carries the reproductive cells–the spores. A structure for carrying the spores–the *Hymenophore*–forms in a position which varies according to the species and from this gills, tubes or similar members are differentiated, in the case of the cap fungi, usually radially.

The main parts of the hymenophore are an inner layer (the *gill-trama* or *tube-trama),* formed from the trama-hyphae and, on each side of this, a branching zone of the hymenial fascicle termed the *sub-hymenium,* and, finally, the spore-bearing layer or *hymenium.* On this spore-bearing layer are innumerable spore-bearing structures *(Basidia)* or spore-containers *(Asci),* arranged pallisade-wise over the surfaces of grooves and folds, gills, tubes, or spines. Between these may be present supporting or nutrient filaments called *Paraphyses* and larger, single-cell tubes, the *Cystidia.*

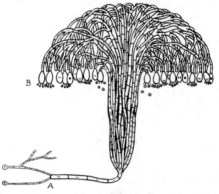

Fig. 2: Development of the fruit body of a cap fungus

The main conditions – apart from light, air, water and warmth – for the formation of the fruit-body are, even to-day, insufficiently understood. This is why the cultivation of most fungi under natural conditions is still very rare and, under the artificial conditions of a laboratory, is only possible up to the formation of mycelium and without any possibility of developing fruit-bodies. Many wearisome experiments will have to be carried out and repeated in laboratories before, even in the case of one species, all the biological conditions are right for the fungus to grow to the spore-bearing stage, or even to the formation of the fruit-body.

Experience shows that very dry winds, sharp frosts, or prolonged rain or drought can hinder or prevent the growth of fungi. However, if the climate and the local weather conditions are right, if there is sufficient moisture in the air, and if the ground is at a suitable temperature, the mycelium, on suitable ground rich in nourishment, can develop astonishingly quickly, using the excess of nourishment to form more thickly-matted tissue and, finally, the beginnings of the fruit-bodies.

Under the microscope the embryo fruit-bodies show as minute webs or knots of hyphae and soon become visible to the naked eye as little round lumps, at first the size of a pin-head, with stem and cap soon becoming differentiated. At this stage already, a surface-layer of thick-walled hyphae, the skin-forming, or *Blematogen* layer is formed. In cross-section this differs from other tissue in having thicker hyphae walls, less compact coiling, and in being more susceptible to dye. This forms the various types of veil, which may be membranous, gelatinous, or slimy. These veils are only temporarily necessary. They soon become redundant, and even a hindrance, and so they often soon disappear, leaving only traces or none at all. Thus the fact that they are usually present can only be proved by research into the life-history and development of a fungus.

The various veils and rings of the cap-fungi—the Universal Veil, the Partial Veil, the Ring, and the Volva are often regarded as forming part of the structure of the stem. Some fungi even have a multiple veil. These various organs can only be understood by studying their their development and origin. Already in the earliest form of the fruit-body rudiment the fruit-body proper begins to develop as an inner, more-compact mass of much branched hyphae and a less-compact outer zone occurs, called the Volva or, more accurately, the Primary Peridium. In the gill-fungi, however, there is no primary peridium such as encloses the *Gasteromycetes* (puff-balls), but only inter-connected partial-veils. Since the hyphae of the volva always originate from the part which they afterwards cover one should, in the case of the cap-fungi, really only refer to the cap-volva, stem-volva, etc. However, because of the way they grow together, they give the deceptive impression of being originally a complete veil such as encloses the early stages of the *Phallus impudicus* (Stinkhorn). So it is usual to describe them as apparently complete veils: the 'Universal Veil', and the inner, 'Partial Veil'. For practical reasons we will keep to this nomenclature.

The most noticeable of the veils is the outer covering—the Exoperidium or Universal Veil which encloses the fungus in its earliest stage rather like an egg-shell. This is frequently found and is important to those fungi which exist, either permanently or for a considerable time, underground but is only found as a genuine peridium in later development on the *Gasteromycetes*.

According to Lohwag, the volva is an inheritance from the time when fungi lived underground. It temporarily hinders the expansion of the cap, and brings the Hymenophores (the gills, tubes, or spines), which are growing from the under surface of the cap towards the stem, in contact with the tissue covering the stem so that the growing elements of the cap-tissue, the *Trama-hyphae* and the cap-margin hyphae can grow into it and form a firmer tissue. Germination of these hyphae when they come into contact with other tissues often occurs and can be seen under an ordinary magnifying glass in a vertical

section of, for example, young specimens of the *Amanita muscaria* (Fly
Aganic). As the stem grows longer and the cap opens the veil tears in
a manner characteristic of the species. It must disappear by the time
the spores are ripe in order not to hinder their distribution. The remains are usually left at the base as a sheath and, in the case of several
species, on top of the cap as scales or warts. If these remains are very
small and delicate they can only be seen by the naked eye as minute
scales, or sometimes merely as a silvery sheen. At maturity even these
disappear.

The inner veil – the Endoperidium or Partial Veil – covers the
hymenium from the margin of the cap to the upper part of the stem.
It originates either from the tissue of the margin of the cap – the
hyphae growing out of the margin of the cap uniting with the tissue
of the stem cortex to form a ring – or it originates from the Hymenophore. In this case the Gill Trama grows away from the edge and
unites with the cortical tissue from the upper part of the stem to form
an annular, more or less fine, porous mesh. If the hyphae do not
develop no ring is formed. In some fungi the veil is very fragile and
it is generally so frail that, as the stem elongates and the cap expands,
it tears into innumerable fine scales which cover the stem and so no
longer appear as a ring. It is this fine mesh or network on the young
stems which cause the markings like snake-skin on the stems of some
cap-fungi.

If the inner veil is stronger it will remain even when the cap is
expanded but will break, either at the margin of the cap, or at the
stem, at the time when the spores ripen. If the veil breaks at the cap
margin it will remain firmly attached to the stem in the form of a
collar. This collar is low on the stem, points upwards, has a tattered
edge, and is made of a filamentous, loose tissue. It is called the *Annulus
inferus* or Inferior Ring. If, when the cap expands, the veil breaks free
only at the stem it remains attached to the cap as a tattered fringe (the
Marginal Veil) and does not disappear until later (as in the genus
Naematoloma). When, as happens with some fungi – for example the
Lepiota procera (Parasol Mushroom) – the veil breaks away first from
the stem and then from the cap, it remains as a moveable ring
(Annulus Mobilis) attached, rather like a serviette ring, to the stem.
If the edge of the cap is inrolled no ring is formed. Formation of a
ring depends on the curvature of the margin of the cap and the resulting position of the edge of the cap in relation to the surface of the
stem. If it is completely curved inwards the growing hyphae at the
margin of the cap cannot reach the stem. In some species however,
the skin of the cap becomes slimy and then the hyphae of the cap surface can come into contact with the cortical tissue of the stem. The
veil then stretches as a gossamer curtain – the *Cortina* – between the
edge of the cap and the stem. It tears as the cap expands and the very
transitory remains of the gossamer are left on the edge of the cap, on
the stem, or on both. These are often so slight that they can only be

seen if coloured by spores which have dropped on to them.

In some *Amanita* species, which at first have bell-shaped caps with even edges, the longtitudinal axis of the gills is parallel with the stem. the free ends of the Hymenophores are in contact with each other and grow, almost throughout their length, with the volva of the stem. If the stem now elongates and the cap expands, the veil, except for a small strip, breaks free from the stem and is lifted up by the cap. If it lifts slowly on the edge of the cap away from the edges of the gills it will hang downwards from the top of the stem as a wide frill. This higher, different type of ring, is called the *Annulus Superus,* or Armilla. It is a ventilating tissue consisting of air-filled tissue elements.

As a result of this completely different origin of the ring it will be understood why this is grooved. As it tears from the edges of the gills the impression of the shape of the hymenium – that is of the lines of the gills – is left in the form of channels or grooves on the upper part of the stem and of the ring. That is why the edges of the gills of some fungi appear, under the microscope, to be floccose. Under the microscope it is clear that they are composed of the same tissue, and of the same types of hyphae, as the ring. The hyphae cells which have become detached are cystidia. The network pattern and the flakes on the stems of some *Boleti* are of the same origin. These are also rudimentary hymenial tissue, that is, continuations of the tube-layers formed from the tubes which were continuous with the stem of the fungus in its earliest stage. As a result of the elongation of the stem this tissue is stretched, in the form of a network, longtitudinally, and when the stem thickens, is torn into scales or flakes.

The veil (in the cap- or stem-volva form) may also swell completely or partially as a result of absorbing water, becoming jellified or moist, and finally completely slimy, leaving a slimy surface on the cap, or a slimy ring or veil which then disappear on maturity.

An actual 'division of labour' seems to be necessary among the tissues which participate in building up the fleshy fruit-bodies, full of sap, and often large and bulky, which grow so quickly and often seem to shoot up out of the ground. This is especially noticeable in a system of guide strands which sometimes approximates to the arrangements in the highly-developed seed plants. These specialised types of hyphae are the vascular-hyphae and the thread-hyphae.

The vascular-hyphae conduct the nutrients and large quantities of water. In doing so they swell considerably, the cell walls thicken, with dissolution of transverse cell walls where necessary, and strengthen themselves against pressure by circular or spiral thickening. In this way they function very like the sieve-tubes of the seed plants. The purpose of the thread-hyphae is to strengthen and protect the guide-vessels mechanically and in this way they are similar to the schlerenchyma of the flowering plants.

The stem of a fungus has a cortical layer, a medullary layer, and, as its main substance, body-tissue with ground-, growth-, and nutrient-hyphae. Its main purpose is to raise the fruit-body sufficiently far out of the sub-stratum—more-or-less above the surface of the ground—to enable the spores to be deposited unhindered.

This condition imposes its shape. When the fungus is very young the stem is still quite short and thick, often nearly spherical, and still more-or-less attached to the undersurface of the cap. With further growth it elongates, severs its attachment to the cap and its append-ages, and attains the length typical of the species. At the same time the original spherical shape changes and it becomes cylindrical, evenly thick or bulbous, sometimes narrowing above, and often bulbous at the base. It is usually central to the cap but is sometimes attached excentrically. When growing among tall plants, or in grass or moss, it is often clustered and multicapped. If growing between stones or the roots of a tree, it may grow longer than is necessary for a single cap growing on level ground. On the surface it appears smooth or rough, sometimes also striated, scaly, silky, granular, or with a flour-like, downy surface. Internally, it may be firm and solid, hollow, pithy, stuffed or fibrous, elastic or tough, soft or brittle. It may often retain until maturity traces of its underground development in the form of a veil or ring, scales or grooves, snake-skin markings or tufts on the stem.

The forms the fruit-body can take are extremely varied. Most common is the cap. But the fruit-body also repeats many other shapes in nature. It can be globular, star-shaped, antler-shaped, bush-like and branching, bulbous, disc-shaped, shell- or ear- shaped, like a tongue or liver, bracket-shaped, or lobed. It can form cups, vessels, or discs and may be flat or umberella-shaped, with or without a stem. It may have one cap or several and the single cap may be spherical, hemis-pherical, bell-shaped or conical, convex or flattened-convex, concave or funnel-shaped, domed, with a central hump like the boss of a shield —called an *umbo*—with wave-like curves, or inturned.

There may be a variety of surfaces: matt or shiny, smooth or rough, warty, with tubercles or spines, wrinkled or furrowed, puckered or veined, streaked or grooved, occasionally zoned, bare or matted, fibrous, felted, or downy, scaly or tufted. Its consistency may be hard or soft, fleshy or tough, filled with sap or dry, woody or skinny, leathery or jelley-like, waxy or cartilaginous, firm or slimy to watery.

Fungi show an astonishing variety of colours and it is almost im-possible to describe all the various shades. These can only be conveyed satisfactorily be really sensitive paintings.

Their variety of colour is only exceeded by the variety of different and delicate flavours, varying from the most unpleasant to the most excellent. Equally varied are the different odours, from the most delightful to the most disgusting.

Taste and smell can be very important, and sometimes essential, in order to recognise a species. Here it should be noted that the scent they give off is sometimes quite different from that of the juice which can be pressed out of them. Some quite odourless fungi can provide strongly-smelling oils which may be obtained by treatment with water or with weak alkalis, or again, a fungus may have a smell on one type of ground which is quite different from that on another.

THE SPORES

The fruit-bodies of fungi – the caps which we collect – play a vital part in their life-cycle since it is these which produce the spores and ensure their dispersal. The spores are cells, varying according to the fungus species, which become detached from the mother plant and which can grow independently into a new fungus. Thus they have the same function as the seeds of phanerogams. It must be remembered, however, that spores and seeds have entirely different origins.

The shape, size, and colour of the spores are characteristic of the various varieties and species of fungus and are sufficiently constant and unalterable to serve as a means of identifying the species. They are microscopically small, measuring only a few thousandths of a millimetre. In measuring spores the unit is the Micron, equal to $1/1,000$ millimetre and denoted by the Greek letter Mu (μ).

In shape they may be elongated, egg-shaped, round, angular or star-shaped. Their surface can be smooth or rough, granular, warty, or prickly. Many spores have a definite superficial ornamentation. Sometimes they are glassy, colourless and transparent (Hyaline). In the mass they then appear white. More usually they have a very definite colour. Because of the extreme variations in other characteristics of fungi the spores provide the most effective way of distinguishing the species and so microscopical examination of the spores is essential to any scientific study.

The colour of the spore dust may be black, olive-brown or other shades of brown such as violet- or purple-brown, red-brown or tawny; often various shades of yellow from a rust-yellow to ochre, golden-yellow or cream to whitish; sometimes rust-red, flesh-pink, or pink. Apart from the fact that each observer has a different impression of the various shades of colour and their description it is almost impossible to specify a really practicable colour scale. In practice, the spore colour can often be noted while the fungus is growing. If they are in clusters, or growing above others, the lower caps or stems are often powdered with spore dust from those above.

At home there is a very simple way to ascertain the colour. Simply cut off the stem close to the cap and lay the cap, with the fruiting layer (gills, tubes, etc.) downwards, on a sheet of white paper (if the spores are white or light in colour the paper should be dark-blue or black). Cover the cap with a glass or dish and leave for six to eight hours or overnight. The spores will drop and form a spore-pattern on the paper showing, not only the colour of the spores, but also the arrangement of gills or tubes in relation to the stem. The spore dust is very easily blown away but a permanent record can be made by spraying it with a painter's fixative, or by using specially prepared spore-paper. The paper should then be dried, either in the air or by warming carefully, and pressed lightly under blotting paper. This makes a permanent record but, as spores which have been fixed in this way may darken slightly, some unfixed spore dust should also be kept in an envelope. For purely scientic purposes, especially for classification, the 'amyloid' reaction of spores is very important. This means the property of membranes, in this case of the spore- or hyphae-membranes, to colour blue in an aqueous solution of Potassium iodide, Iodine and Chloral hydrate ('Melzer's Iodine').

CLASSIFICATION

The various considerations affecting fungus classification can here only be dealt with briefly.

The larger fungi form two main groups: the Ascomycetes and the Basidiomycetes. Ascomycetes (ascus = sack) are so-called because their spores, the ascospores, are developed within a sack- or tube-like structure, the ascus. Since this contains the spores it is also known as the sporangium (Fig. 3, below). The ascus may develop on any part of the branches of the mycelium, or on special parts of the fruit-body consisting of tissues of interwoven fibres (plectenchyma) which, together with non-fertile, nutrient threads (paraphyses) form, in a palisade-type of arrangement, a fruiting-layer – the hymenium.

Fig. 3:
(much enlarged)

a
Asci (the sacs with
Ascospores)

b
Basidia (the club-shaped cells
with Basidiospores)

The Basidiomycetes (basidium = club) are fungi whose spores develop, not in containers, but on the outside of specialised organs. These are usually club-shaped, single-cell structures at the ends of the hyphae, called Basidia (Fig. 3). The spores are then known as Basidiospores. The Basidiomycetes occur in various forms, with and without fruit-bodies. They consist largely of sterile plectemchyma tissue and, like the ascomycetes, form palisade-like patterns together with the non-fertile paraphyses and cystidia (undeveloped basidia in various stages of development) producing a fruiting body–the hymenium. As terminals of conducting channels the cystidia presumably function as organs of secretion. Basidia and Asci are similar structures (homologous). Since, as Lohwag proved in 1937, Basidia developed from Asci and the Basidiomycetes from the Ascomycetes, it is not surprising that they develop in a similar manner forming colonies and fruit-bodies (hymenia) on which they are side by side in clusters or palisades. These layers develop into exposed-spored (gymnocarpous) or enclosed-spored (angiocarpous) fruit bodies. As these types of fruit-body are the only ones which can be seen with the naked eye, the Asci and Basidia which are developed from them are called the 'principal fruit form'. The other forms of spore development, which remain unknown to all except experts, as, for example, the Conidia, are called the 'secondary fruit form'. Thus, from the point of view of their origin, the formation of a special hymenium is common to the Ascomycetes and the Basidiomycetes.

It is in this way that Nature solves the problem of creating and distributing an astronomical number of spores from a small space. A mature fruit-body of the common Field Mushroom *(Agaricus campestris)* disperses 16,000 million spores. The *Polyporous squamosus* distributes 50 milliard and the Giant Puff Ball, *(Lycoperdon giganteum)* a total of 7 billion!

Since the fruit layer occupies every part of the surfaces of the fruit-body–all the grooves and ridges of the gills, tubes, or spines, the limited available space is enormously increased. In the Ascomycetes the Asci are in a flat fruiting layer within the fruit-body which, at maturity, bursts through the apex of the fruit-body. In the Discomycetes, or disc-fungi, this fruit layer forms an *Apothecium,* that is a cup-shaped structure with the Asci exposed on its surface. The chief representatives of the disc-fungi are the Morels, the genus *Helvella (= Gyromitra),* and the cup fungi. The Truffles *(Tuberales)* are bulbous or spherical with internal hollows or passages containing the fruit layers.

The two main groups of fungi are subdivided as follows:–

Protoascomycetes (comprising the simpler *Ascomycetes* and the *Saccharomycetes* or yeasts), and the

Euascomycetes (the more-highly organised *Ascomycetes*). These are again divided into six Orders, distinguished by the shapes of the fruit bodies:

1. *Plectascales,* fungi with closed, globular fruit-bodies, e.g. the moulds such as *Aspergillus* and *Penicillium* and the mildews *(Erysiphaceae).*

2. *Pyrenomycetales,* fungi with the spore-bearing surface within an urn- or jug-shaped perithecium open at the top, e.g. the *Claviceps purpurea* (Ergot).

3. *Discomycetales,* Disc fungi with the spore-bearing layer open on the surface of a cup- or dish-shaped fruit-body which may sometimes also be folded and irregularly lobed. Among these are the Cup Fungi, Morels, and the Helvella species.

4. *Tuberales,* the Truffles, in which the spore-bearing surfaces are in passages and spaces within the bulbous, underground fruit-body.

5. *Exoascales,* microscopically small parasites without fruit-bodies, e.g. the species of the genus *Taphrina* which cause the 'Witches' Broom' deformity on trees.

6. *Laboulbeniales,* microscopically small parasites with bristle-shaped fruit-bodies without a spore-bearing layer. They live on insects, e.g. the *Stigmatomyces Baeri,* which ingests live ground beetles.

The majority of the Ascomycetes are microscopically small. They are important since they cause various plant diseases but they can only be studied under the microscope. The amateur collector will, in practice, be interested only in the third and fourth Orders, the Disc Fungi and the Truffles, since these include some excellent edible species as well as poisonous ones.

The Basidiomycetes consist of five Orders. These are:

1. *Hymenomycetes.* Most of the finer looking cap fungi belong to this order. They have undivided basidea and fruit-bodies with exposed spore-bearing surfaces.

2. *Gasteromycetes.* These include the Puff Balls and Earth Stars. They also have undivided basidia but closed fruit-bodies.

3. *Auriculariales.* These include the 'Jew's Ear' *(Auricularia auricula. Hirneola)* which grows on old elderberry bushes among others. These have basidia divided horizontally into four, and jelly-like fruit-bodies.

4. and 5. *Uredinales* and *Ustilaginales.* The Rusts and Smuts. These have horizontally-divided, or undivided, basidia but no fruit-bodies. These are microscopically small, but are of great economic importance since they are parasitic on grain and cause disease.

In practice, the amateur collector will be chiefly interested in the first three of the above Orders which can be seen with the naked eye.

The *Hymenomycetes*–with a large number of species and, for the amateur collector, the most important Order–have the basidia in a clearly-defined fruit layer between the innumerable ridges of the hymenium (gills, tubes, or spines). They are usually on the under-surface of the cap, which is at first enclosed and, in the *Gasteromycetes,* within the fruit-body.

The *Hymenomycetes* are again subdivided according to the various types of fruit-bodies. Firstly, there are the Gill Fungi *(Agaricales)*. The gills–familiar to everybody from the common mushroom–are very numerous, thin as a knife-blade, and run radially from the edge of the cap to the top of the stem. They are usually separate from each other throughout their length. The gills are either crowded close together or relatively free from each other. There are often long and shorter gills or long ones alternating with short gills from the edge of the cap which do not reach the stem. Frequently they are considerably, or slightly, branched or forked or, more rarely, transversally joined at the base (anastomosing). In section the gills may be simple and undivided, or notched. They are sometimes differently coloured from the spores.

A distinguishing characteristic of a species, although this does vary with the development of the cap, is the way the gills are attached to the stem (Fig. 4, below). When they just touch the top of the stem they are said to be adnexed. When the whole width of the gills is attached to the stem they are adnate. If there is a curve inwards towards the stem (when the inner edge of the gill is slightly concave) they are sinuate. If the gills do not touch the stem they are called free, and when they run a short distance down the stem they are decurrent.

Fruit-bodies with a spore-bearing layer of fleshy, usually detachable, tubes instead of gills are the *Boletaceae*. These were formerly placed among the *Polypores* but are to-day definitely counted as *Agaricales*. Unlike the *Polypores* they do not develop their fruit-bearing layer until their growth, and their final form, is complete but development is then rapid. An exception is the *Armillaria mellea* which can develop basidia even when the mycelium has already emerged above ground.

The *Polypores* (Bracket Fungi), another important family with many species, have their fruit-bearing layer as a connected mass with many thickly-clustered, tube-like, or honey-combed depressions, usually on the under-surface of a cap- or bracket-shaped fruit-body. Excluding the *Meruliaceae*–with flat folds, or ribs–(well-known examples being the *Serpula lacrimans*, *Merulius*, better known as 'Dry Rot', and the *Fistulina hepatica*, the Beef Steak Fungus–with

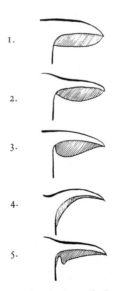

Fig. 4: Attachment of the gills, 1. Adnate, 2. Adnexed, 3. Free, 4. Decurrent, 5. Sinuate

different, free-standing tubes)–there still remain many fine-looking fungi among the *Polypores*. They are of very varied shapes, usually growing on trees, with leathery, corklike, or woody, fruit-bodies, both with and without stems.

In addition to the more impressive cap-fungi, there are, in the woods and fields, vast numbers of microscopically-small fungi which may be noticed because of their striking shapes and colours. To go into detail about these interesting and enormously varied fungi is outside the scope of this book. Quite specialised knowledge, as well as a microscope, are essential for their study. However, a brief survey of the development of the fruit-forming structures and the spores may be interesting.

Among the lowest, that is the mono–cellular, organisms the entire fungus body is transformed into a reproductive structure. This is known as the holocarpic form. In these, the mycelium and the fruit-body develop consecutively in the same organism. In other fungi this development is hidden because the two developments are separated both in space and time. Only a part of the vegetative body, of the fungus matrix or of the mycelium, is used in the development of the reproductive organs while the remainder continues to be devoted to the original purpose of nourishment. This part of the mycelium remains underground while the other part is continually growing towards the air and light. These forms of fungi, differentiated into vegetative and reproductive parts are known as 'eucarpic'.

The simplest form of spore formation is when the hyphae break down into single cells. These break away from each other, often dispersing to great distances, and may, somewhere and sometime, grow to new hyphae. These single cells are known as Oidia. They are equivalent to germinating cells, from which they only differ in that they originate, not from shoots but from the breakdown of a cell. The transition from this stage to an actual spore is unnoticeable. They are either differentiated from ordinary hyphae or they originate from special spore bearing-structures. If these spore-bearing structures develop the spores within special cells (endogenous) these are called Sporangia. If these spores live in water they are mobile, flagellate 'Zoospores' resembling single-cell animal organisms. If they live on land, have a membrane, and do not move, they are called 'Sporangiospores'. If, however, the spore-bearing structures release the spores externally, they are Conidiophores and their spores are Conidia. Especially tough, thick-walled Conidia are called Chlamydospores or, like the permanent mycelia, they are also known as Gemmae.

In the case of the larger fungi the Conidiophores unite to form larger cell-colonies, the fruit-bodies. If these are grouped together as a sheaf they are known as Coremia but if they form flattened layers they are called, in the case of saprophytes (i.e. fungi living on decaying organic matter) Sporodochia, and with parasites, Acervuli. The tissue from which they come is known as the Stroma. If the condiophore

1. THE DEATH CAP, *Amanita phalloides* (left) p 61
2. THE DESTROYING ANGEL, *Amanita virosa* (right) p 62

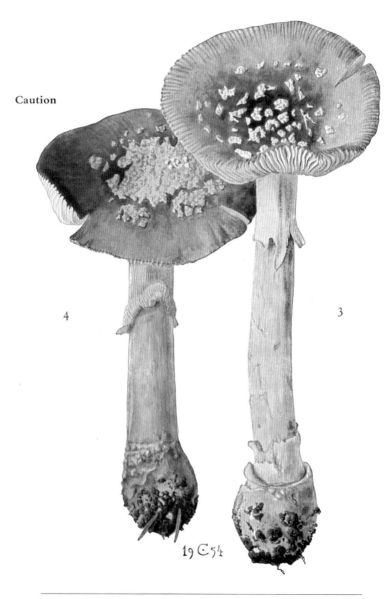

Poisonous

Caution

4

3

19 C 54

3. *Amanita pantherina* (right) p 64
4. *Amanita spissa* (left) p 65

hyphae unite to form a capsule or vessel in which the spores are enclosed these capsules are known as Pycnidia and the spores, Pycnidiospores. Depending on their type of formation they are called, if formed by division and growth of a single terminal hypha, meristogenous. If formed from several interwoven hyphae of different origins they are symphogenous. Between these types there are transitional forms due to lack of nourishment. With sufficient nourishment all these different forms of spores can be formed on any part of the mycelium. If a species is able to develop several of these spore forms it is called pleomorphous. Another group of spore forms is determined, not by the nourishment, but by sexual developments in the cells. These can survive in unfavourable conditions.

REPRODUCTION

In order to understand this chapter, intended especially for those who want to go more deeply into the lives of fungi, it is advisable to refresh the memory on a few botanical principles.

All higher organisms—including the fungi, as well as the higher plants and animals—are composed of cells. The cells, which are the basis of all living things, consist mainly of cell-protoplasm and the cell-nucleus, which is the 'brain' of the cell. Characteristic of the nucleus are special thread-shaped bodies called, because they can be dyed, Chromosomes (Greek: *chroma* = colour, *somas* = body). The chromosomes are mainly responsible for inherited characteristics. (For the sake of completeness it may be mentioned that carriers of inherited characters have also been found in the cell plasma.) The number of chromosomes, which always occur in pairs, usually several pairs in a nucleus, is constant and characteristic for each species.

Thus every normal cell in the body of every animal has two 'sets' of chromosomes and the cell-nuclei containing these two sets are known as diploid. However, the cells which serve for reproduction have only one set of chromosomes and are known as haploid. This is obvious if the fact that the number of chromosomes in the normal cells remains constant is remembered. If the generative cells had double sets, the union of these would produce four sets, and of these eight sets, and so on. So, in order that the number of chomosomes should remain constant it is necessary that the generative cells should have only half the normal number. Then, if two such haploid, generative cells unite the resulting organism will have the normal two sets of chromosomes in all the growth cells, which are then diploid. The reduction from double to single sets in the generative cells is brought about by a complicated process of nuclear division known as Meiosis and it is the result of Meiosis which produces the haploid generative cell.

C

This diversity of cells with double and single sets of chromosomes also occurs in the plant kingdom. Here, however, the situation is complicated by the fact that not merely the generative cells can be haploid but also complete phases in the life history of the plant. For example, the entire plant of the moss is haploid—it represents the haploid phase—and only the sporophores which rise from it with minute stems (except for the tiny cap) are diploid. These represent the diploid phase in the life-cycle of the moss.

In the development of fungi—in the cell nucleus as well as in the mycelium and fruit body—the same characteristic change of phase occurs. Here there is also a haploid phase with one set of chromosomes, and a diploid phase with two. The haploid phase terminates with fertilization, the union of the nuclei, or Caryogamy, and the diploid phase with the 'Reduction Division' (Meiosis); that is, with the return to a single set of chromosomes. In addition to this change of nuclear phase, and parallel with it, there is also a morphological change, comparable with the change of form between the mosses and their sporophores.

A few decades ago it was not even known that fungi reproduce sexually. To-day every student knows this but much patient study and experiment was needed before the process could be elucidated.

The Ascomycetes can reproduce asexually or vegitatively by setting free the young cells, the Exospores or Conidia, from special filaments of their mycelium—the Sporangia. These are spores covered by a membrane which are produced by cellular division (e.g. the moulds— *Aspergillus.)*

Ascomycetes can, however, also reproduce sexually. In this case, special sex structures, the male Antheridium and the female Ascogonium are formed on their mycelium. In some species, the female organs have at their apex as a terminal cell, an auxilliary organ in the form of an elongated, arched papilla—a multicellular protruberance—designed to entwine, and so often snakelike in shape—the Trychogyne. When the bulbous, multi-nuclear, male antheridium attaches to the bladder-like, multi-nuclear, female ascogonium the dividing membranes between the two disappear and the contents of the antheridium enters the ascogonium. If a trychogyne is present the contents enter the ascogonium through this. The nuclei of different sexes pair together—known as plasmogamy—but are still far from uniting. After the two nuclei have divided simultaneously, the pairs of nuclei, one female, one male, move into sack-shaped, branching cell fibres, the ascogenous hyphae. With the majority of the ascomycetes, there are then formed at the tips of the terminal cells, special backward-bending continuations forming a stalked hook. The pair of nuclei move into the bend of these hooks and divide conjugally several times, i.e. a male and a female nucleus simultaneously. Of the four daughter-nuclei two, of different sex, remain behind in the cell tip, one of each moves to the apex of the hook and to the stalk. Hook and stalk now become separated from the top downwards by horizontal walls (septae) as a result of which a three-celled structure with two single-nuclear cells and one double-nuclear cell is formed. The double-nuclear cell is the Ascus, in which the two nuclei now finally unite to form one large nucleus. This is the stage of the fusion of the nuclei, or cariogamy. The cell grows to a bulbous, still mononuclear ascus, or sack. In three further consecutive divisions eight nuclei are produced around which, by free cell formation by membranes, eight haploid spores, the ascospores, are formed. They remain longtitudinally in line, like peas in a pod, usually in eights, embedded in the remaining cellular fluid (Epiplasma) which has not been used up. (Fig. 3, p. 22). In the meantime, after the transverse membrane has opened, the hook cell has fused with the stalk cell and passed its nucleus into this. As a result, a double-nuclear fusion cell is also formed here which can also produce a new ascus. Thus, completely sympodial, branched bunches of asci are formed at each end of an ascogenous hypha filament. These unite with sterile filaments, the paraphyses, to form superficial spore-bearing layers or hymenia. On maturity, the asci disperse their spores explosively at the least disturbance or, when moist, as a result of swelling in the sun's heat, and the spores are dispersed by the slightest breeze. If a ripe cup fungus is picked in the Spring, this spore explosion can be seen as a cloud of fine dust.

The reproduction of the Basidiomycetes is very similar. The basidio-spores are ambisexual. When these germinate, a germination mycelium, also called primary mycelium, is formed, and from this, by repeated cell division, a mycelium with entirely mononuclear cells of the same sex as the spores from which it originates. It remains almost indefinitely capable of growth. Sex organs are not recognisably formed on it. But when two mycelium branches meet and fuse, their nuclei pair together. Their cell fluids (plasma) unite but, strangely, their nuclei do not fuse for some considerable time. A cell now germinates on a lateral branch of the zygote, which is the product of this fusion of plasma, into which the pair of nuclei move. This subdivides repeatedly into paired-nuclear branches and becomes a paired-nuclear mycelium. The curious process of division which occurs here is the equivalent of the hook formation of the ascomycetes (Fig. 5). Beside the twin nuclei, a lateral continuation of the cell is formed, also hook- or horn-shaped and arched downwards—a so-called 'Clamp Connection'—into which a nucleus moves and divides. The second nucleus

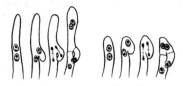

Fig. 5: Hooks and clamp-connections as homologous structures

of the pair remains in the clamp connection while the first moves towards the tip. In the meantime, the second nucleus has divided inside the cell. One of the two resulting daughter-nuclei moves towards the tip of the cell, the other moving backwards towards the lower part of the cell. Between these two daughter-nuclei, immediately under the point of attachment of the clamp-connection, a lateral membrane (septum) is formed, and a second membrane (in the clamp-connection itself) divides this from the terminal cell. The terminal cell (the nucleus of the clamp-connection) thus receives a pair of nuclei of different sex. But the base cell (the original cell) also develops two nuclei as a result of the nucleus from the apex of the clamp-connection moving into this cell through an opening formed for this purpose. The terminal cell goes on growing, and the formation of clamp-connections is repeated with each division of a pair of nuclei so that a profusely-branching, completely double-nuclear (dycaryotic) 'clamp-mycelium', with a clamp-connection at each septum is formed. The hooks of the Ascomycetes and the clamp-connections of the Basidiomycetes are both diversionary in purpose and hinder the mating of sister-nuclei. In this form the mycelium can go on growing for years until certain definite external conditions cause profuse branching and inter-lacing of the hyphae to form bundles and from these, the embryo-fruit bodies, fruit-bodies with double nuclei are developed.

Thus, in contrast to the Ascomycetes, the tissue (Plectenchyma) of the Basidiomycete fruit-bodies consist of hyphae with two nuclei (dicariotic). In their hymenial layers which, in the majority of species, are found on the under-surfaces of the fruit bodies, the terminal cells of the hyphae swell and become tuberous basidiae. (Fig. 3, p. 22). It is only in these that the two nuclei finally fuse. This is the stage of Caryogamy (nuclear fusion) and, as a result of three further divisions, four haploid nuclei – that is, each with one set of chromosomes – are formed. As a result of this, the inheritable characteristics of the paternal and maternal nuclei are shared in such a way that each new nucleus receives a part of each. One each of these daughter-nuclei forces itself through four or two (seldom more) thin, short, filaments or stalks – the sterigmae – which have in the meantime grown at the tips of the Basidiae, into the globular to egg-shaped Basidiospores which are maturing at their ends. The spores are finally ejected by elastic expansion of the cell walls and dispersed by the slightest current of air (which may occur through the higher temperature within the fruit-body), and are finally further dispersed by the wind.

PRACTICAL ASPECTS

COLLECTING FUNGI

Finding edible, or any of the larger, fungi depends very much on the season of the year and on the weather. There seems to be nothing as temperamental, and so little subject to any recognisable laws as the occurence of fungi. Years when they appear in such profusion that it is impossible to collect them all are succeeded by years when even the more common varieties simply do not appear at all or are only found as very poor specimens. However, surprisingly enough, their place is then often taken by otherwise rare species which then grow quite abundantly.

In a good year the harvest can begin as early as April. Morels and False Morels (various species of *Helvella)* may appear simultaneously with the St. George's Mushroom, which takes its name from St. George's Day, 23rd April. These may then be found abundantly, especially in fields near woods and streams, in parks, and among bushes. Occasionally even, the first Edible Boletus *(Boletus edulis)* may appear in May, and perhaps also the first of the poisonous *Inocybe patouliardii,* which may be pure white like champignons, or mealy-yellow, or soon turn red. It is not until June that the *Boletus edulis* appears in any quantity, sometimes with other of the brightly-coloured Boleti, such as the *Boletus luridas,* remaining for only two or three weeks and then disappearing completely until late Summer or even until September. If the weather is suitable, June or July bring out the Common Mushroom, as well as the Fairy Ring Champignon—the latter often in rows or rings—as well as the first of the Russulas, and several other species. If the Summer is dry and hot there will be relatively few fungi, but rain and mist at the beginning of September, extending into October, will bring out the Russulas and Boleti and other species in really large quantities. By mid-October, with the first frosts, most of the Boleti disappear, but they are succeeded by many of the late-Autumn species which are unaffected by quite heavy frosts: the *Collybia butyracea, Tricholoma terraem, Tricholoma nudum,* and several others.

Some species are at their best at this time of the year and are found in considerable quantities, among these the *Tricholoma portentosum,* the *Clytocybe agregata* and the *Hygrophorous hypothejus.* Then also, a few specimens of *Boletus edulis* and of *Boletus erythropus* may survive in sheltered spots until quite late in the Winter. By this time, the average amateur collector will feel that the season is over. However, for real enthusiasts who know where to look and are not expecting large quantities, but who are hoping for rare or unusual specimens, this can be the best time. Even in snow the *Collybia velutipes* and *Pleurotus ostreatus* may be found in some quantity.

For collecting fungi, the best container is a light, well-ventilated basket, preferably with a sliding cover. Other containers, such as boxes or paper bags, are only suitable if they are pierced for ventilation. Fungi need air and should not be allowed to become warm since heat and moisture speed up the decomposition of their proteins and they are then soon spoiled, while dangerous poisons—ptomaines such as occur when fish or meat go bad—are then formed. Sacks or bags are not really suitable for carrying fungi, and paper bags can only be used temporarily and for small quantities.

At home, however tired one may be, it is worth taking the trouble to empty the basket and spread out the fungi, preferably by species. If the worst of the dirt has already been removed when they were gathered, the final cleaning and preparation for cooking can, if necessary, be left until the next day. However, if everybody is still feeling bright, sorting and identifying the bag can be pleasant and exciting.

To avoid damaging the delicate mycelium and spoiling future crops, fungi should never be pulled out of the ground. They should be twisted, and then very carefully lifted to preserve the stem. Beginners, especially, should avoid cutting the stem. It is important, from the beginning, to learn the characteristics of the whole fungus and, if they are not carefully lifted, a good deal of the stem, with the volva, may remain in the ground. Important characteristics will then often be overlooked, and there may be confusion with similar, but poisonous, species.

The fungus should then be roughly cleaned with a knife and dirt, pieces of foliage, or maggots, removed. It can then be seen at once whether the specimen is old, spongy, and maggoty, or worth taking home. Old, watery, mildewed, or maggoty specimens are better left to shed their spores and fertilize the ground. Specimens which are only slightly maggoty should have the maggot-holes cut out and should then be stored separately; otherwise they will very quickly spoil the rest. Experienced collectors can tell at a glance whether a specimen is worth collecting and will leave those not in good condition to deposit their spores. If the stem is tough, fibrous, or woody, only the cap should be collected. Roughly cleaning and preparing the fungi in this way while they are being collected makes it much easier to prepare them for cooking later on and saves a good deal of time and work in the kitchen.

Most fungi grow in colonies because the mycelium produces a great many fruit bodies. So, when you come across an edible fungus, it is worth looking around carefully because there will probably be one or two others of the same species growing nearby. If, when you are hunting for them, you remember which species grows in which kind of wood and on what ground, you are much more likely to be successful. Apart from knowing as much as possible about their habitats, it will be useful to keep in mind what is known about the formation of mycorrhiza and the association of fungus mycelium with the roots of trees while, if you also know something about Fairy Rings, you will be a step ahead of the average beginner and it will all help in the search.

It is worth getting into the habit of walking slowly and, instead of merely looking at the ground, observing the trees and the whole woodland scene as well. You may come across fungi growing on the trees, as well as beautiful lichens and mosses, and the delightfully-coloured species of the tiny, 'lower' fungi. Then there may well be a wealth of small animal life–bees, ants, insects, spiders, dragon-flies, frogs, snakes, squirrels, mice, moles–the very existence of which you only vaguely imagined before.

To return to fungi! At first it is best to keep to those edible fungi which you know already or which are easily recognised, especially if they are plentiful and worth collecting. As for those species which you do not yet know well, it is better, for the time being, to keep to those which are growing plentifully. In any case, beginners should be content at first to confine themselves to a few species. It is much better to get to know a few varieties really well than to gather quantities of different species which can never all be learned at once. The next time, study one or two other species, and so learn gradually, but thoroughly.

From the very beginning, it is important to acquire the habit of studying every part of a species which you know in order to be able to recognise it again in its different stages of development. In this way it will be remembered, and will provide a basis from which the variety of different characteristics will be enlightening instead of confusing. From the very beginning it is also important to study the surroundings, and the plants and trees growing nearby. A good knowledge of the habitats of the various species will prevent many wasted hours of search before finding enough to take home to cook. If you have the chance to go out with an expert you will learn more in the one expedition than in years of study. However, books *are* useful, and even essential, to those who want to learn more than merely a few of the best-known, edible species. A basic grounding in botany is very useful, as well as a good magnifying-glass and, if possible, a microscope. At first, it will be encouraging enough, if there are not too many more mistakes than correct identifications. But certainty and confidence will come with practice.

USELESS FUNGI?

Nothing in Nature is useless. In the scheme of things, creatures or organisms which, because we do not know their purpose, seem useless to us, are often very important. It is enough to mention those invisible but active organisms which fertilize the soil and so provide us with our daily bread. There is reason and purpose, even for poisonous fungi, as there is for dangerous or poisonous insects, or for beasts

of prey, and nothing in Nature can be destroyed without upsetting
the balance. So it is a pity to destroy any fungus wantonly. What may
seem worthless to an amateur may be very valuable indeed to an
expert.

Many of the fungi which we come across, indeed the majority, are
not good to eat. Only a few are poisonous, but they may be flavour-
less, more-or-less bitter, acrid, or peppery as well as tough, or woody.
Taste or smell may be uninviting, yet not a few of these, even if they
cannot be eaten, can be used for flavouring. Even bitterness, or a peppery flavour, are gastronomically useful and we should be sorry to
be without them. To be used in this way, for flavouring, a fungus
must first be dried and ground to powder.

Many other species, even those which we avoid as poisonous, have
little-known, healing properties of which Penicillin (p. 57) is only
one example.

SMALL AND LITTLE-KNOWN FUNGI

Very small, or tiny fungi are hardly worth considering from the point
of view of edibility, except perhaps by a few experts, and if they
happen to appear in such quantities as to make them worth collecting.
For mycologists, however, these, and the barely-visible micromycetes are among the most interesting and still provide opportun-
ities for new discoveries.

There are hundreds of species of fairly small fungi which only confuse beginners and are not very easily identified by experts. From the
point of view of edibility, most books used to list these as 'edibility
unknown'. To-day, most of these have been tried and their edibility
investigated. Experts who really know these fungi will, even in the
poorest season, always be able to find something to take home to
cook but the articles about them are mostly dispersed in the journals
of the various botanical societies and still need collating.

Not a few young people first become interested in fungi out of
curiosity or start by collecting them for cooking and then take up
Natural History seriously. Those who are seriously interested would
be well advised to join the nearest Botanical Society. Lectures and
practical work in the field, in company with other enthusiasts, as well
as a good library will all help to stimulate and increase their knowledge.

AMATEURS AND MYCOLOGY

Microscopically small fungi, the micromycetes, can be found
throughout the year, Winter included. They can be exceedingly
interesting, but the results are of purely scientific value and success in

Poisonous

Caution

5

6

19 C 53

5. THE FLY AGARIC, *Amanita muscaria* (left) p 65
6. THE BLUSHER, *Amanita rubescens* (right) p 66

7

7. THE GRISETTE, *Amanita (Amanitopsis) vaginata* p 67

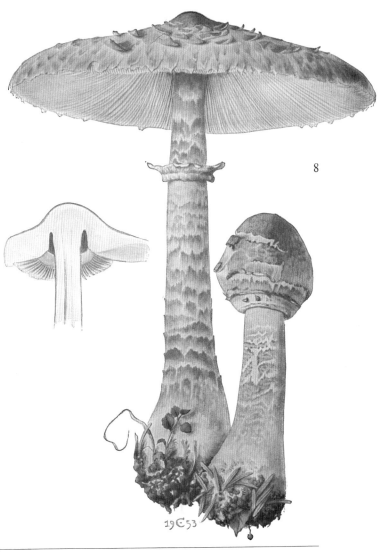

8

8. THE PARASOL MUSHROOM, *Lepiota procera* p 69

9. ST. GEORGE'S MUSHROOM, *Tricholoma gambosum* p 70

Edible

10

Edible

11

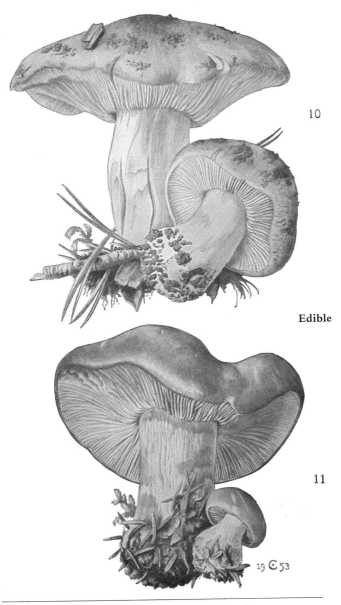

19 Ⓒ 53

10. *Tricholoma flavovirens (equestre)* (upper) p 71
11. *Tricholoma (Lepista) nudum* (lower) p 71

Edible

13

Caution

12

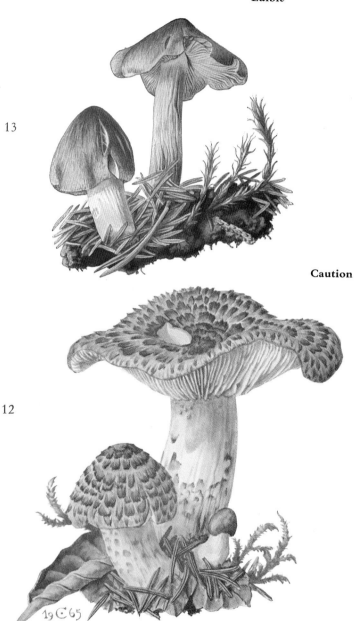

19 C 65

12. *Tricholoma pardinum (tigrinum)* (lower) p 72
13. *Tricholoma terreum* (upper) p 73

14

14. *Clitocybe nebularis* p 73

Edible

15

19 C 53

15. THE HONEY FUNGUS, *Armillaria mellea* p 74

studying them is only possible if the work is undertaken scientifically and with a good microscope as the minimum essential equipment. To avoid disappointment it is advisable to have expert help and advice. Classification, for instance, is very definitely a matter for experts and even the classification of the many species of gill-fungi requires years of study and experience. Few people are suited to this work. However, even an amateur with little experience can help to clarify many important details if he combines careful observation with exact, accurate description. Among the many matters which amateur mycologists can clarify are, for instance, local and popular names for fungi, and details of habitat and plant geography – that is, information about distribution, and about species of fungi and other plants growing in association with trees.

EDIBLE OR POISONOUS?

There is only one answer to the frequently-repeated question: are there any general rules for telling whether a fungus is edible or poisonous? The answer is No! There are definitely no general features which distinguish one from the other. So there can be no possible rules, any more than there are to distinguish edible from poisonous seed plants. Just as the deadly nightshade and other dangerous plants have to be learned individually, it is equally essential to learn the details of the various fungi individually in order to know which are poisonous and which are edible.

With fungi there is the added danger of ancient superstitions still being believed and this danger is likely to continue until children are taught at school to recognise at least the few common dangerous species. Is it too much to hope that teachers in children's schools should be expected to be able to recognise at least the Death Cap in its various stages of development?

I still remember the horror with which I heard an elderly, and otherwise capable, teacher confidently repeating to a gathering of thoroughly-educated people that old-wives'-tale which claims that you can tell a poisonous fungus because it will turn a silver spoon black when cooking. Even with my experience, it was not easy to convince these people that this was dangerous nonsense. Even now, I and my friends find that this superstition is still believed, as well as other, equally ridiculous, ones as, for instance, that salt sprinkled on the gills will infallibly reveal a poisonous fungus by turning yellow! This is all rubbish, of course, and these incorrect ideas are more dangerous than complete ignorance.

When and why should a silver spoon, cooked with fungi, turn black? The blackening of a silver spoon depends on the content of sulphur – containing protein of the fungus. Any dish containing eggs will also discolour silver, due to slight separation of hydrogen sulphide producing on the silver object a thin layer of yellow to brown silver sulphide which appears black if the layer is thick enough. This has nothing at all to do with poison!

The fact that a fungus may be eaten by some animals or insects such as maggots, beetles, centipedes and snakes without harming them is no proof that it would be safe for us to do so. Investigations have shown that game, and many other animals, can eat fungi, including the poisonous ones, without any ill-effects and can gradually increase their tolerance to the poison. Guinea pigs are scarcely affected by the poison, and rabbits have anti-toxins in their stomachs and brains which enable them to eat even Death Caps without danger. (Dr. Limousin of Clermont-Ferrand has based a special treatment of Amanita poisoning on this fact. It consists in feeding to the patient a brew made from finely-chopped, raw, rabbits' stomachs and brains. Unfortunately this is said to be quite ineffective.) Of our tame animals, the pig is least affected by poisonous fungi and is said to have an anti-toxin in its stomach which breaks up the poisons into harmless components.

Considered without regard to other features, no shape or colouring, and no special smell or taste can indicate whether a certain fungus is poisonous or safe to eat. The only safety lies in learning exactly how to distinguish the poisonous species. Some deadly-poisonous fungi can be quite beautiful, smell pleasantly and, if they are eaten, have quite a good flavour. On the other hand, some decidedly-unpleasant looking fungi, with 'poisonous looking' colours–perhaps colouring even more unpleasantly when bruised–with a far-from-pleasant smell and–at least when raw–an unpleasant taste may yet, if properly prepared and cooked, be excellent to eat and completely harmless. Then again, some only mildly-harmful fungi may cause quite a lot of discomfort and sickness immediately after eating, while the most dangerous one of all–the Death Cap–leaves the victim feeling perfectly well and happy after eating it and it is only after many hours, too late for treatment, that the first, terribly-unpleasant symptons appear.

Then again, some of the deadly-poisonous species deceptively resemble some well-known, and very good, edible species. Again, some fungi which, from the point of view of taste and wholesomeness, are very nearly as good as the *Boletus edulis* may colour when bruised to dirty-brown, light- or deep-blue, green or red, purple to violet, or even inky-black, without in the least spoiling their edibility, taste, or wholesomeness. As a criterion of edibility, colour is more deceptive than any other characteristic.

Colour changes in fungi, when they are touched, cut, or bruised, are due to the presence of phenol-type compounds (carbolic acid and similar compounds) and their oxidation by the oxygen in the atmosphere. Some Lactarius species, especially *Lactarius sanguifluus* and *Lactarius deliciosus* and many Boleti, especially the *Boletus luridas,*

Boletus scaber and *Boletus versipelli*: are well-known to students for changes of this kind and yet (in Germany) are feared, almost super-stitiously, by the country-people on account of these changes. Colour changes never indicate that a fungus is poisonous; they merely show that a certain fermentation-process is taking place. They also depend on the number of nutrient-hyphae present in the flesh.

Generalisations are always wrong and any rules, which might apply to a few species about which it is possible to generalise, should be accepted with caution.

FUNGUS POISONING

Poison may be defined as a substance which, when introduced into a healthy or living organism, in small or even in minute quantities, is destructive or deadly in its effect. In a wider sense, poison is also anything which, even though not taken in large quantities, has a harmful effect on the organism. So it is often the case that it is only the quantity, or the sum of the quantities taken, which make a sub-stance poisonous. Thus frequent or daily use of otherwise harmless things like the various spices used in cooking, quite apart from coffee, tea, tobacco, and alcohol can have harmful consequences.

Depending on the physiological effect of the poison on the various organs of the body we speak of a poison as affecting the stomach, intestinal tract, heart, blood, or the nervous system. Poisons in the last group, because they damage the individual cells to a greater or lesser extent, are also referred to as protoplasm poisons. Depending on the result, we speak of slight or serious poisoning. Fungi can cause serious, or deadly, poisoning but also quite minor cases involving no more than localised, mild indigestion. A substance can have a poison-ous effect on the digestion of a child or of an old person, or on some-body already weakened by illness, while being quite harmless to a healthy, vigorous adult. Susceptibilty to poison varies enormously with the individual. Nobody is quite immune, certainly not all the time. However, there are individuals who are nearly immune to cer-tain poisons including those of fungi. This resistance to poison can be acquired by habit over a long period in the same way as lifelong, heavy smokers, or heavy drinkers, in spite of the quantities of alcohol they consume, may live to a ripe old age.

In classical times people were already enquiring into the origins of fungus poisoning. The Greek, Dioscorides, a doctor of Cilicia about the middle of the 1st-century AD believed, (as also Pliny, and even Albertus Magnus, who copied from him) that fungi became poisonous through growing near rusty iron, decaying rubbish, near snake-holes, or near a tree with poisonous fruit! Put in this way, this is, of course, nonsense. Yet there is a grain of truth in it, inasmuch as the substratum, the sap of trees, and the composition of the soil,

including any artificial additives, can influence the flavour and the
food value, if not also the wholesomeness of fungi; quite apart from
the questionable effects on them of artificial manure or poisonous
waste-products from factories. It is possible that even such a first-class,
edible fungus as the Common Mushroom might acquire poisonous
characteristics in this way, as also the smell of carbolic, or the inky
taste which have sometimes been detected in other edible species. At
least bitterness and acridity may well, to some extent, depend on
where the fungus grows. Equally, geographical differences in fungi
are probably due, not merely to climate, but also to differences in the
composition of the soil.

Mildly poisonous fungi usually cause merely gastric disturbance–
more-or-less serious sickness, giddiness, stomach pains and diarrhoea,
the symptoms usually occuring quite soon after eating the fungus.
Purging and evacuation is soon followed by recovery, and this is
usually complete within a few days, though often leaving a decided
antipathy to all fungi which may last for some time.

Serious fungus poisoning, which can endanger life, unfortunately
only reveals itself after a considerable incubation- or latent- period.
This may last for several days and, in the case of a poisonous fungus
found in Poland (p. 43), even as long as 17 days. When an illness is
delayed as long as this, the usual first-aid remedies–emetics and
laxatives–will probably be ineffective. A doctor should be called at
once, or the patient should be taken to a hospital, since this is more
likely to be equipped to treat the case effectively at this stage.

Doctors, and people experienced with fungi can usually deduce
from the circumstances the probable cause of poisoning or the
species of fungus involved. Symptoms of poisoning are as different
as the poison content of the various fungi but they do depend on the
amount swallowed, the age of the patient, and the state of the
digestive system. Children are more susceptible than adults and a
person already ill may be completely prostrated by quite small
quantities. However, if a perfectly healthy person, soon after, or
sometime after, a meal develops sudden sickness (often when asleep),
or serious sickness with cholera-like diarrhoea, cramp, increased
flow of saliva, watering at the eyes, nerve pains, sensory or visual
disturbances, signs of jaundice, breathing difficulties or heart trouble,
with or without loss of consciousness, then, at any rate during the
fungus season, the possibility of fungus poisoning must be considered.
A doctor should be called in any case and, in the meantime, the patient
should be given an emetic and a laxative. If animal charcoal is
available this may prove very useful in absorbing the poison. Any
remains of the meal, as well as the matter brought up by the patient,
should be saved for investigation. Further treatment is a matter for
the doctor, but first aid should be given before his arrival though its
effectivness will depend on the degree and type of poison.

Atropine (the poison found in deadly nightshade), and Ringer's

Solution (physiological salt solution of Common Salt) with grape sugar, given as sub-cutaneous injections, have been found to be of great help in the most serious cases of poisoning. It is not advisable to rely on the 'Limousin Treatment' (p. 36). Modern therapy includes adrenal hormones and Vitamins B. and K. Attempts to provide the body with immunity to fungus poisoning by means of an anti-phalloidal serum have not yet proved to be reliable although recent research is tending in this direction.

The following is a list of the most dangerous species. (The numbers indicate the number of the Description.)

Cortinarius (Dermocybe) orellanus★

Amanita phalloides (1), the Death Cap–and its closest related varieties: *Amanita verna* (1), and *Amanita virosa* (2)

Inocybe patouillardi (19), as well as some other species of Inocybe

Amanita pantherina (3)

Amanita muscaria (5), and also its brown and yellow varieties: *Amanita regalis, Amanita umbrina,* and *Amanita formosa* (5)

Gyromitra esculenta (69)

Boletus satanas (54)

Gyromitra gigas (69)

Rhodophyllus sinuatus, lividus (23)

Clitocybe dealbata,

Clitocybe rivuloso,

Tricholoma tigrinum (12)

Lepiota helveola, and a few other rare small species of Lepiota.

Agaricus xanthodermus, (the Yellow Staining Mushroom) (24)

Agaricus (meleagris) placomyces (24)

A few other species are either poisonous or suspected of being so but these are extremely rare, or have so far only been found abroad.

Details are given below of typical symptoms of poisoning which may occur after eating the various dangerous species. If more than one species is eaten, the symptoms may be the sum of those caused by each or may, sometimes, cancel each other out. The most dangerous poisons are those which are insoluble in water and unaffected by heat.

According to Th. Wieland, *Amanita phalloides, Amanita virosa,* and *Amanita verna* contain Phalloidine, Amanitine, and also the hitherto-unknown, and highly poisonous, Phalloine. Two hundredths of a milligram of Amanitine will kill a mouse, and a forkful of the cooked fungus–that is, a medium cap, or 50 grams–is enough to kill an adult person. Much smaller quantities are deadly to children. It is this dangerous poison, which enters the blood stream only after leaving the alimentary canal and then begins its destructive effect on the kidneys, liver, and the circulatory system, which is responsible for the delayed recognition of poisoning. In its effect it can be compared to a delayed-action bomb! The first symptoms appear–

★ Not as yet found in Great Britain. (Translator's note.)

after a so-called latent period—at the earliest 5-10 hours, generally 19 hours, and sometimes not until 30-48 hours, after the fateful meal. By then it is sometimes much too late for effective countermeasures.

The typical symptoms of Amanita poisoning are: sudden and severe attacks of sickness with severe diarrhoea, colic-like pains in the stomach, cramp in the legs and weakness of the heart, disturbed circulation with gradual cardiac paralysis, swelling and extreme sensitivity of the liver, blood and albumen in the urine, and internal hemorrhage. The patient remains fully conscious during this period and, if it has not occured sooner through heart failure, death occurs in from two to twelve days as a result of damage to the liver (coma hepaticum).

With any of the above symptoms a doctor should be called at once. Treatment usually consists in the administration of substances which absorb the poison, such as animal charcoal (recently Carbogel) and stimulation of the heart with Coramine or Cardiazol. The serious loss of water and salts is countered by injection of Ringer's Solution with grape sugar. Further remedies are Insulin, blood-transfusion, adrenal hormones, and Vitamins B. and K. The Limousin-Treatment (p. 36) is now outmoded.

The *Gyromitra esculenta* (69), and the closely related *Gyromitra gigas* were formerly regarded as excellent and good to eat. It is only recently, after considerable discussion that they have been classed as poisonous and it has now been proved that they have caused numerous deaths among adults, and still more among children.

The *Gyromitra esculenta* especially, was sold in German markets and, although not quite so good to eat as the *Morchella esculenta* (the Morel), was very popular. Because of its danger (the poisonous effect does, actually, seem to vary according to the district, the climate, and other circumstances) it has now been withdrawn from public sale. There are, it is true, certain essential rules for preparing this fungus. It must be simmered in water for at least two minutes and the water thrown away, then very thoroughly dried, and eaten only once in the course of a day. As these precautions were frequently disregarded it became essential to class it as poisonous.

The well-known poison, Helvellic acid, seems to be combined with another poison, similar to that of the *Amanita phalloides*, which attacks the circulatory system. In any case, serious damage to the liver and to the organs of the circulatory system have been proved. The first symptoms may occur, typically, quite early or quite late, within two to four, or twelve, hours after eating the fungus. There is serious sickness, cramp, loss of consciousness, jaundice, and pains in the region of the liver. Death may occur from two days, to two weeks, after these symptoms, due to damage to the liver (coma hepaticum). A doctor should be called as soon as the symptoms occur. He will send the patient to hospital and treatment is similar to that for Amanita poisoning.

The *Inocybe patoulliardii* (19) has only been known to be deadly poisonous for the last 40 years, this recognition being due to fatalities in Munich and elsewhere in Germany. It is dangerous because it is fairly common and, if the differences are overlooked, can be mistaken for the common mushroom. It contains 150-200 times as much Muscarine as the *Amanita muscaria*! Its poison attacks the nervous system, especially the brain, and also the secretory and autonomic nervous systems, the nerves, that is, which control the secretory and unconscious actions of the body. The symptoms are typical, and are luckily soon apparent. They begin, 15-45 minutes after eating the fungus, with severe sweating, watering of the eyes, sickness, and stomach pains. The face becomes red, there is shivering, the pulse is slow, and blood-pressure falls. The eye-pupils contract, the eyes are staring, and the sense of sight diminishes to the point of temporary blindness. There is no diminution of consciousness and no symptoms of intoxication as with *Amanita muscaria*. Sickness and diarrhoea are usually slight. If the heart holds out, or if only a small quantity of the fungus was eaten, recovery soon follows. Otherwise death occurs through cessation of respiration or through heart failure. With these symptoms, a doctor should be called immediately. He will probably send the patient to hospital. Treatment includes emptying stomach and intestines, heart stimulants and, frequently, sub-cutaneous Atropine injections.

A number of other related species of Inocybe are also dangerously poisonous, but luckily these are mostly small and unattractive.

The *Amanita pantherina* (3), and the *Amanita muscaria* (5) contain poisons which stimulate or paralyse the nervous system. The first of these contains the poison Muscarine, which has to-day been largely investigated, but this is only one of the poisons and not the most important. *Amanita muscaria* contains a form of atropine named muscaridine. Whether *Amanita muscaria* also contains muscarine, and whether other unknown poisons are also present, still remains to be investigated.

Luckily for the patient, typical symptoms appear 15-30 minutes after eating. The patient is highly agitated as though intoxicated, seems to suffer from a temporary form of madness with delusions, impaired memory, and attempts to talk with non-existent people. There is delirium, laughter, screams, attacks of frenzy, with cramp, muscular spasms, profuse flow of saliva and watering of the eyes, affected vision and temporary blindness, disturbed diction, and finally, giddiness, sleepiness, loss of consciousness, and contraction of the eyes. The pulse is slow and weak, or barely noticeable. The poisoning is only fatal if there is inability to breathe or weakness of the heart. A doctor should be called if any of these symptoms appear. Pending his arrival, emetics and laxitives should be given, to empty stomach and intestines. The doctor may prescribe tea, coffee, and heart stimulants and give subcutaneous injections of Ringer's solution and atropine.

Amanita muscaria is used as an intoxicant by a number of tribes in Siberia. The intoxicating element is secreted by the kidneys and goes, almost completely, into the urine. This is not only preserved by the owner for his own use, but is also drunk by others who intoxicate themselves on it.*

Rhodophyllus (Entoloma) sinuatus, lividus (23) There has been some doubt as to how dangerous this fungus is. It has undoubtedly been responsible for serious gastric illness with vomiting, but it has probably not caused any deaths.

The *Boletus satanus* (54) eaten raw, or insufficiently cooked can cause serious and long-enduring vomiting and diarrhoea. Although no case of death from eating this fungus is on record, it must be regarded as dangerously poisonous.

The *Tricholoma tigrinum* (12) is, on the whole, so uncommon that there is luckily little opportunity of getting to know it from personal observation. Although not necessarily deadly poison this fungus does cause, quite soon after eating, serious vomiting, long-lasting gastric disorder, and such a long-lasting general weakness of the entire body that it must be included among the most dangerously poisonous fungi. For anybody with a weak heart it can be indirectly fatal. Medical attention is essential.

Tricholoma pessundatum: authorities differ as to whether this species is edible or poisonous. It is safest to regard it as very suspicious and to avoid it.

Clitocybe dealbata and *Clitocybe rivulosa*: both these species – frequently found close together – must be regarded as poisonous.

There are also various small, little-known, white species of Clito-cybe which are dangerous or doubtful and the above list must not be regarded as exhaustive. However, to extend the list of doubtful or suspicious species would serve little purpose. It cannot be too strongly urged that fungus hunters should never attempt to eat any species at all unless they are certain that they recognise and know it, or unless it is recommended to them by an expert.

The number of slightly poisonous, or not quite harmless fungi should not be underestimated and so it is wise to keep to the 150-200 edible species and to make ones selection from among them. There are plenty of good, safe-to-eat species to be found and to concentrate on finding the best of these which may be growing in your neigh-bourhood is enough to keep most enthusiasts fully occupied.

Some fungi are decidedly dangerous if eaten alone in sufficient quantity to make a meal, yet quite safe in small quantities eaten with other species, or if used in small quantities for flavouring. For example, *Lactarius helvus*, or the *Scleroderma vulgare* (the Common

---

* According to tradition, the Vikings ate *Amanita muscaria* in order to attain their moods of fighting frenzy known as 'going berserk'. Robert Graves in the Foreword to '*The Greek Myths*' (Penguin Books, 1966) suggests that the Centaurs of mythology ate *Amanita muscaria* and adds: "I now believe that 'ambrosia' and 'nectar' were intoxicant mushrooms, certainly the *Amanita muscaria,* but perhaps others too, especially a small, slender dung-mushroom named *Panaeolus papilionaceus,* which induces harmless and most enjoyable hallucinations." (Translator's note.)

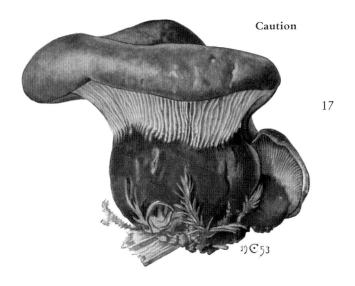

Caution

17

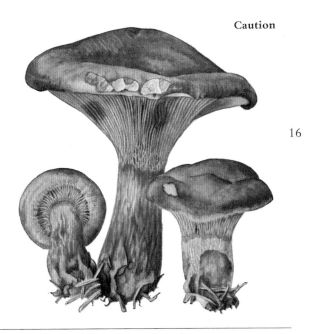

Caution

16

16. *Paxillus involutus* (lower) p 75
17. *Paxillus atrotomentosus* (upper) p 75

18

18. *Flammulina (Collybia) velutipes* p 76

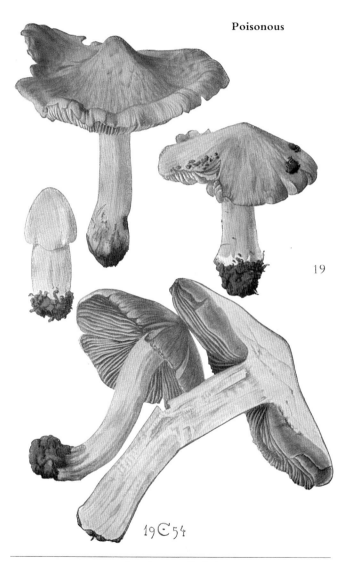

19

19C54

19. *Inocybe patouillardii* p 77

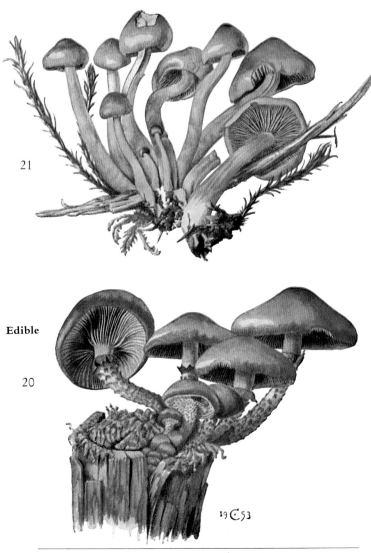

21

20

20. *Pholiota (Kuehneromyces) mutabilis* (lower) p 77
21. *Hypholoma capnoides* (upper) p 78

Earth Ball) are poisonous to some people, yet perfectly safe if used in small quantities for flavouring.

A few fungi have the curious property of causing poisonous symptoms if eaten with alcohol. Especially the *Coprinus atramentarius*, otherwise safe and good to eat, causes nausea if alcohol is taken with it or soon afterwards. The same thing occurs with the *Boletus luridus*. From recent personal experience, I must especially warn anybody with a weak heart against taking alcohol, even in small quantities, after eating the excellent *Boletus luridus*. Serious symptoms, which dangerously affect the circulation, may occur even after 24 hours.

Recently, a practically unknown fungus, hitherto probably known only to a few experts who were unaware of its danger, caused great alarm in Poland. A sudden outbreak of widespread poisoning alarmed doctors and mycologists. This was due to a fungus with a brown to orange cap, the *Cortinarius (Dermocybe) orellanus,* belonging to the large genus Cortinarius, of which none of the wide variety of species was then known to be poisonous. Its effects were reminiscent of an infectious epidemic and presented a hitherto-unknown type of illness ('Orellana Syndrome'). This fungus is dangerous both to people and to animals. It often causes serious damage to the kidneys and a typical feature is the long incubation-period (2-17 days), so that any possibility of fungus poisoning is often overlooked. In 1952, 1955, and 1957 132 cases, of which 19 were fatal, were observed clinically in Poland.

In earlier German books on fungi, quite a number of species have been classed as poisonous, or suspicious which have since been recognised as edible, or else as quite harmless. But the principle– never to class a species as edible without completely reliable evidence that it is safe–should still be followed. It is better to describe one fungus too many as dangerous rather than to classify a questionable one as safe.

DETOXIFICATION

Although vinegar, common salt, or a pinch of soda do, to some extent, neutralise slightly poisonous or indigestible fungi it is wise not to place too much trust in this. This is especially the case if the fungi are being used for a salad–and all the best edible species, including the delicate Russulas and one or two of the genus Paxillus, are excellent for salads. Unless absolutely certain that all the species being used are completely harmless raw, they should first be well-simmered in water, or steamed. A single *Russula emetica*, for instance, included by mistake in a salad made of the edible Russulas, can cause thoroughly unpleasant consequences, but first stewed in water, it is quite harmless.

However, the really poisonous species, such as the Death Cap, the dangerous *Amanita pantherina*, and the Inocybes are not made any safer by soda, or by prolonged stewing and discarding the water. The

D

really dangerous and deadly fungi cannot be neutralised by cooking
or drying, and nobody is immune to them.

RAW FUNGI

Some fungi, which are excellent and harmless when cooked, are
either indigestible, or even possibly poisonous, when raw. Many,
especially all the Morels, the Helvellas, the Pezizales (Cup Fungi), as
well as all the Paxilli, the Clavarias, and all the red-spored Boleti
may possibly be dangerous to health if insufficiently cooked, or
merely lightly fried.

The following are often poisonous when eaten raw:

All the Amanitas, including those known to be edible such as
Amanita rubescens, Amanita spissa and *Amanitopsis vaginata.*

All Boleti with red spores (luridi) – *Boletus erythropus, Boletus
luridus,* and related species.

All species of Hydnum and Sarcodon,

The Parasol Mushroom,

All sharp or acrid Russula and Lactarius species,

Of the milder Russulas, all species with tough flesh.

All Paxilli, since these soon decay,

All Clavarias, especially the beautiful *Clavaria (Ramaria) formosa*
and the pale *Clavaria (Ramaria) pallida.*

The *Armillaria mellea* and the *Clitocybe nebularis,*

The *Craterellus cornucopioides* (Horn of Plenty)

All Helvellas (with these the cooking water should be discarded),
Morels,[1] and the Cup Fungi are – on account of their wax-like, rather
gristly consistancy – difficult to digest unless they are cut into small
pieces. Their particular acids and juices help to make them indigestible
and their many folds and grooves render them liable to decay. When
they are no longer quite fresh, their decomposition products may
perhaps do more harm than the acids they are known to contain.

Thus fungi can only be recommended raw with considerable
reservations. Even the *Boletus edulis* may sometimes produce ill effects
if eaten raw. Best suited for raw eating are the *Lactarius volemus,* the
Russula vesca and the *Russula cyanoxantha,* but even these,[2] uncooked,
should be eaten in small quantities. The great majority of all fungi
are, when raw, if not poisonous either unsatisfactory in flavour, or
not very wholesome. Even the best of the edible fungi can only be
regarded as really easily digestible if carefully prepared and cooked.
People with very sensitive digestions should perhaps not eat fungi

---

[1] The author is here presumably addressing himself to those with extremely
delicate digestions. It is not normally considered necessary to chop-up the
much-prized Morel *(Morchella esculenta)* although these should be trimmed,
very well washed, and parboiled before further cooking.

[2] In addition to these, the Common Mushroom and young Puff Balls, as well
as Truffles, are excellent raw in salads. (Translator's note.)

at all, or should have them cut into small pieces before cooking. None of their nutritive value will be lost and their taste and digestibility improved. Often enough, however, it is the variety of other things eaten and druck at the same meal which help to make the best fungi seem indigestible.

IMAGINARY POISONING

It is not only after eating poisonous fungi that discomfort or illness may be experienced. Ignorance of the right way to prepare them, and neglect of the ordinary rules of hygiene and cleanliness, can cause gastric trouble which is at once put down to fungus poisoning when it is nothing of the kind. To eat a very large quantity of a perfectly edible fungus, or to swallow large pieces without properly chewing them, may naturally cause trouble. Old, wet, or dirty fungi, if carelessly kept, will go bad fairly quickly and become dangerous before they begin to smell unpleasantly.

It is safe enough to eat dishes of warmed-up fungi on the same day, or even on the day following their first cooking provided they have been kept in a refrigerator or reasonably cool, but they should not be kept longer than 24 hours.

It is also perfectly safe to eat fungi which, in late Autumn or Winter, have become frozen provided they are in good condition when thawed. Otherwise they can be dangerous.

Species which may be found in the late Autumn and Winter are:
Lyophyllum decastes (= *Tricholoma aggregatum*)
Hygrophorous hypothejus,
Hypholoma capnoides,
Laccaria laccata,
Tricholoma (Lepista) saevum, personatum,
Tricholoma terreum,
Collybia butyracea,
Clitocybe (Cantharellula) cyathiformis,
Tricholoma portentosum,
Flammulina velutipes, Collybia,
Pleurotus ostreatus.

It happens not infrequently that people imagine, quite incorrectly, that they have been poisoned by a fungus. The only remedy against this kind of imagination is a really good knowledge of fungi, especially of the dangerous species.

It is quite a different matter in the case of allergy or personal idiosyncracy–the extreme, illogical dislike felt by some people for certain foods, whether strawberries, apples, fish, or shell-fish. This illogical distaste has a psychological origin and is more frequent in women (especially when pregnant) than in men. To disregard this is is wrong and can lead to suffering. So nobody–and this applies to children–should be forced to eat fungi against his will.

FUNGI AS FOOD

Fungi provide us with useful additions to our diet in the form of proteins, carbohydrates, and valuable salts and vitamins. As food their value is somewhere between meat and vegetables and is certainly equivalent to the best vegetables. They are thus well suited to provide extra nourishment for diets which lack protein and in this sense they have rightly been called 'the meat of the woods'. Their contribution is also important from the point of view of flavouring. The diversity of their flavours and their value as a relish have been recognised from the earliest times. Nobles paid high prices for fungi; they were delicacies for princes; praised by poets; and bought and sold in the markets for high prices. On the Continent, a special code of law was formulated to deal with the search for truffles, and dogs, pigs, and bears were trained for this. In the Middle Ages the better fungi, the so-called 'Noble Fungi' had to be collected and presented periodically to the reigning prince or to the nobles. Only much later, when the knowledge of edible and poisonous fungi had been nearly lost, (and had to be rediscovered by botanists and a few interested doctors) were fungi referred to in depreciatory terms as 'Jews' Meat' or even 'Toads Dirt'.

Composition and nutritive-value of fresh fungi
from Bötticher (König), 1950

	Water	Nitrogen	Fats.	Carbohydrates	Fibre	Ash	Calories per
	%	%	%	%	%	%	100 gm.
Common Mushroom	89.70	4.88	0.20	3.57	0.83	0.82	26
Chanterelle	91.42	2.64	0.43	3.81	0.96	0.74	21
Lactarius deliciosus	88.77	3.08	0.76	3.09	3.63	0.67	22
Marasmius oreades	83.37	6.83	0.67	6.06	1.52	1.55	41
Boletus edulis	87.13	5.39	0.40	5.12	1.01	0.95	33
Collybia butyracea	92.63	1.48	0.27	3.95	1.22	0.45	17
Boletus luteus	91.63	0.96	0.58	4.27	1.80	0.76	18
Hydnum repandum	92.68	1.79	0.34	3.47	1.03	0.69	17
Helvella esculenta	89.50	3.17	0.21	5.43	0.71	0.98	25
Morel	89.95	3.28	0.43	4.50	0.84	1.01	25
Truffle	77.06	7.57	0.51	6.58	6.36	1.92	44

The values given here can vary considerably according to habitat and stage of development of the fungi. These figures date from some little time ago when it was probably usual to remove the gills or tubes –just the parts richest in protein, which is the chief nutrient found in fungi.

As an example of the food value of fungi it may be mentioned that a German General, Lettow-Vorbeck, hemmed-in with his troops in German East Africa in 1918, managed to save them from starvation and to hold out for some months against superior forces by encouraging them to supplement their meagre rations with whatever fungi they could find.

Not to know and eat fungi is to miss one of the gastronomic pleasures of life, for fungi are not only nourishing but also a delight to the gourmet. First however, the following tables are intended to show what is known about the value of fungi as food.

The proteins in fungi are considered difficult to digest. This is true if the fungi are poorly cooked or, in the case of certain species, are not first sliced. Correctly prepared they are 70% to 80% digestible as shown by the following table.

Protein-Digestibility of Fresh Fungi

	Total Protein %	Digestible Protein %	Digestibility %
Common Mushrooms ...	5.94	4.82	88.5
Puff Balls...............	5.37	4.00	74.1
Clitocybe	2.99	2.64	87.7
Lactarius	2.18	1.71	78.2
Cantharellus clavatus.....	2.69	2.10	79.2
Cantharellus cibarius	1.87	1.38	72.2
Boleti (except B. edulis) ..	1.74	1.38	77.9
Tricholoma.............	1.60	1.08	70.0

This table shows that the Common Mushroom and the Puff Balls, each with more than 5%, are definately rich in protein. Boleti, Tricholomas, and *Cantharellus cibarius*, with less than 2% each, are definitely poor. (The Parasol Mushroom is also especially rich in protein with 5.6%.) Among the Boleti, the *Boletus edulis* with 5.39% is an exception. As far as digestibility of the nitrogenous substances is concerned, the fungi with less protein seem to be less digestible. The Chitin, which forms the cellular membranes, is an indigestible residue. In fungi this takes the place of the cellulose present in other plants and, as an intestinal stimulant, is probably not without value.

A comparison between the protein content of fungi and that of other food is shown below.

Comparative Protein Content
according to Bötticher (Lintzel)

	Total protein in dry mass %	Digestible protein in dry mass %
Meat	83.7	82.8
Common Mushrooms	51.9	45.9
(Boletus edulis and Parasol Mushrooms, similar)		
Puff Balls..................	48.5	35.8
Clitocybe	32.9	28.8
Spinach	34.5	25.0
Legumens	26.3	23.4
Cantharellus clavatus.........	27.7	21.9
Lactarius	26.1	20.4
Tricholoma................	24.3	17.0
Chanterelle	22.8	16.6
Boleti (except Boletus edulis) .	20.0	15.6
Rye Bread	10.7	9.0
Potatoes...................	8.0	7.3

Fungi have a not-inconsiderable carbohydrate content, especially of the sugars, mannose and trehalose. Their fat-content is small and, from the point of view of food-value, unimportant. Their content of enzymes is fairly high, as also of vitally-important minerals, especially of potash, phosphates, manganese, and iron as well as of the basic compounds. Fungi are also very rich in the anti-rachitic Vitamin D, in Vitamin B^1 and B^2, and to some extent in Vitamins A and C.

The following table gives a comparison of the composition and nutritive value of fungi with those of other foods.

Composition and Nutritive Value of Fungi and Other Foods
(Bötticher)

	Water	Nitrogen	Fat	Carbo-hydrates	Fibre	Minerals	Calories 100 grams
Boletus edulis (fresh)	87.0	5.4	0.4	5.2	1.0	1.0	34
Common Mushroom (fresh) .	90.0	4.8	0.2	3.5	0.8	0.8	28
Chanterelles (fresh)	91.5	2.6	0.8	3.5	1.0	0.7	23
Boletus edulis, dried	12.8	36.7	2.7	34.5	6.9	6.4	221

	Water	Nitrogen	Fat	Carbo-hydrates	Fibre	Minerals	Calories/100 grams
Potato	74.9	2.0	0.1	20.9	1.0	1.1	91
Carrot	86.8	1.2	0.3	9.0	1.7	1.0	34
Cauliflower	92.1	1.5	0.1	4.2	1.2	1.9	24
Spinach	93.4	2.2	0.3	1.7	0.5	1.9	25
Asparagus	95.4	1.6	0.1	1.7	0.6	0.6	17
Cucumber	95.2	1.2	0.1	2.3	0.8	0.4	8
Apple	84.8	0.4	—	12.9	1.5	0.5	58
Pear	83.0	0.4	—	12.0	4.3	0.3	56
Raisin	32.0	2.4	0.6	62.0	1.7	1.2	277
Rye Bread	42.3	6.1	0.4	49.3	0.5	1.5	277
Wheat Bread	35.6	7.1	0.5	56.6	0.3	1.1	255
Milk	87.2	3.5	3.7	4.8	—	0.7	62
Butter	13.6	0.7	84.4	0.6	—	0.7	752
Egg	73.7	12.5	12.1	0.5	—	1.1	152
Beef	72.0	21.0	5.5	0.5	—	1.0	141
Veal	72.3	19.0	7.5	0.1	—	1.4	140
Pork	47.5	14.5	37.3	—	—	0.7	380
Liver	71.5	20.0	3.5	3.5	—	1.5	119
Hare	74.1	23.4	1.1	0.2	—	1.2	91
Haddock	81.5	16.9	0.3	—	—	1.2	70
Herring	46.2	18.9	16.9	1.6	—	1.4	167

FUNGI AS ANIMAL FOOD

After what has been said about the nutritive value of fungi it is perhaps superfluous to emphasize their useful possibilities in cattle rearing
and fish culture. Here it may just be mentioned that, according to
Raebiger, who carried out extensive research and practical tests over
many years, fungi can provide valuable food for cattle as an auxilliary
to grazing and normal feeding. The mycologist, Dr. Bötticher, has
also given famers useful advice as to how they may tide over temporary shortages of cattle food by means of fungi. Except for the most
poisonous species, which only pigs can eat without harm, all the
commonly-occurring woodland fungi can be used as animal food.
Especially dried and crushed, and mixed with other foods, they provide a welcome, completely harmless, change of diet for animals.

PRESERVING FUNGI

Fungi can be preserved in various ways: by drying, by making fungus
extract, by salting, by fermentation, by pickling in vinegar, and by
sterilising.

Drying is not only the simplest way to preserve fungi, it is also the best way of maintaining their food value since dried fungi are the richest in calories. The way they have done this from time immemorial in Bavaria is to cut the cleaned fungi into more or less evenly-thick pieces, neither too thick nor too thin, and spread these on boards which are left in the sun. The weather needs watching, and the pieces of fungi must be turned from time to time.

If the weather is bad the fungi are dried indoors, preferably in a large, well-ventilated, dust-free room or, more quickly, in the oven. In the oven the temperature should not be above 140°F. and good ventilation is essential since the fungi should dry evenly and not begin to cook or stick together. They cannot be dried satisfactorily in an oven while other food is cooking as they will be spoiled by the steam given off by the food, remaining sticky and moist, and liable to become mildewed. For room drying, the fungi can be threaded with a needle on to string or twine (knotted between each fungus to prevent them touching) and hung on a suitable frame, or they may be spread on trays or frames of wire-netting, basket-work, muslin or string-netting.

The fungi are sufficiently dry when they feel crisp to the fingers and can easily be broken into powder. It is always worth while making some fungus powder at the same time by pounding the dried fungi in a mortar, or grinding them in a food mill. The powder should be kept in air tight jars and is excellent for seasoning.

Fungus extract can be made by pressing the fresh fungi in a fruit-press or by slicing them finely and heating, with a little salt, over a medium heat. The juice is extracted by filtering, or squeezing through a cloth, and the fungi should be reheated, and the juice extracted, more than once. The extract is then simmered with spices – cinnamon, peppercorns, bay leaves, cloves and salt until it is the consistency of sirop. It should be bottled in air-tight jars and kept in a cool place.

For salting, the fungi can either be washed and parboiled, or fresh, uncooked ones may be used. They are placed in jars with a layer of salt alternating with a layer of fungi. Alternatively, and giving a more even distribution of salt, the fungi can be covered with brine. The jar should be closed, preferably with a wooden cover with a weight on it, and the fungi should always be covered by brine. The jars should be stored in a well-ventilated, cool place (34°–40°F.). A quantity of salt equal to 5–8%, at the most 10%, of the weight of the fungi is sufficient to ensure that they will keep. With this amount of salt, it is then unnecessary, when using the fungi, to soak them in water and doing this extracts the nutritive salts as well as the brine. The salt from the brine can be taken into account when cooking.

Fermentation by means of sour milk (lactic fermentation) is approximately equivalent to making sauerkraut from white cabbage. The fungi are parboiled and then pressed into small, wooden containers or barrels together with $1\frac{1}{2}\%$ salt, $1\frac{1}{2}\%$ sugar, and a little sour

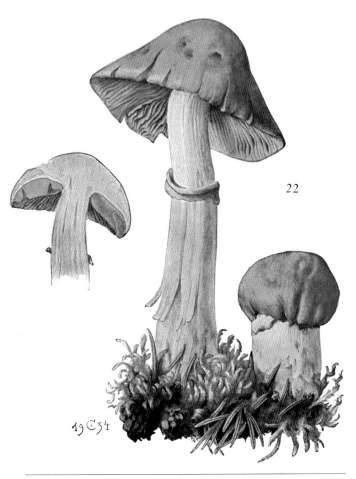

22

22. *Rozites (Pholiota) caperata* p 79

23

23. *Rhodophyllus (Entoloma) sinuatus (lívidus)* p 80

24

24. THE HORSE MUSHROOM, *Agaricus arvensis* p 80

Edible

Edible

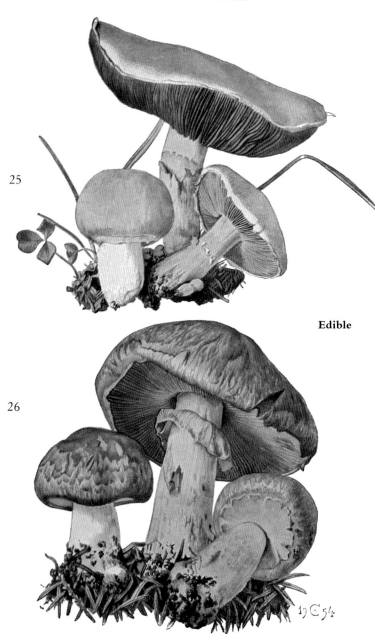

25. THE FIELD MUSHROOM, *Agaricus campestris* (upper) p 81
26. *Agaricus silvaticus* (lower) p 82

milk. The container is then closed with a bung and a liquid, consisting of one part fresh fungus juice to two parts water (or the water in which the fungi were parboiled), is poured in through the bung-hole. During the period of fermentation, which takes 14 days, the barrel must be kept at a temperature between 13° and 18°C. and it must remain full to the bung. When no more foam shows at the bung-hole, the barrel may be closed. It must be stored in a cool place.

This process can also be carried out in any ordinary jar. In that case the fungi must be covered with a clean cloth, and the whole covered firmly with a wooden lid with a weight on it. The lid must always be covered by the liquid. If a mould is formed at the end of the fermentation a quantity of benzoic acid equal to 0.15% should be added to the liquid. The sugar which was added is necessary because fungi do not contain sufficient sugar and without this a satisfactory lactic fermentation is impossible.

At a temperature of 13°–18°C. lactic fermentation begins after 6–12 hours. After first forming a good deal of foam this gradually diminishes after 3 or 4 days, and the process is complete after 8, or at the latest, 14 days. If the container is sufficiently airtight the fungi will keep until the following Spring or early Summer. Preserved in this way they have a pleasant, sharp flavour and can be used exactly as if they were fresh, but they are softer and more digestible. The lactic acid can be, to a great extent, removed by washing, or by soaking in water overnight. Fungi preserved in this way can also be used in salads.

To pickle fungi they should first be simmered in water for 10–15 minutes. (Acid – or sharp-tasting species should first be soaked in water for some time). When cool they are put in a jar and covered with good-quality wine vinegar together with salt, pepper-corns, bay-leaf, cinnamon, cloves, pimiento, tarragon, elderberries and onions – perhaps also with a dash of lemon juice.

The method for sterilising and bottling fungi is the same as for other vegetables and therefore need not be dealt with here. In my experience, it is advisable however, to sterilise fungi twice.

PREPARATION FOR COOKING

The worst of the dirt or impurities should be cleaned off when the fungus is picked. Then, in the kitchen, it should be cut in half and any remaining dirt or sand, leaves or insects this may reveal removed. Any maggoty pieces must be cut away completely, or the good parts carefully cut out. Tough stems should be discarded, unless they are for fungus extract, or for drying and pulverising. The skin should only be peeled if it is slimy, hard, or tough. If it has to be peeled, as thin a strip as possible should be taken off since the skin of the cap contains most of the mineral matter. Gills, tubes, or spines should only be removed if they have become squashed and messy since these are the parts richest in nourishment. The cleaned pieces of fungus are then (if necessary) quickly washed in a sieve, drained, and cut into the thinnest possible slices. Very tough fungi should be chopped into small pieces. In any case it is important to cut the fungus into small pieces, both for the sake of digestibility and also in order that the full flavour of the fungus be obtained. However some gourmets do prefer larger pieces and fungi are also cooked whole for certain recipes, i.e. egg-and-bread-crumbed and fried like a Wiener Schnitzel, or cooked in an omlette.

For cooking, good quality enamelled or earthenware pans should be used, never pans of aluminium, iron, or copper since the metal of these can combine with some fungi to form toxic salts.

As fungi already contain a considerable amount of moisture they should be cooked without water, with a little butter or good-quality fat over a gentle fire. They can be simmered over a low fire for about 15 minutes, with a little chopped parsley or other herbs, and with very little pepper and salt. Then, according to taste, gravy, wine, or a little stock can be added, or they can be scrambled with eggs. For a slightly piquant dish, the fungi can be stirred with a little flour and fat to which vinegar and caraway seeds are added. However, certain fungi have a very delicate flavour and this is lost if too many herbs are used. Digestibility can be improved by adding a pinch of sodium bicarbonate.

In warm weather cooked fungi should be kept in a refrigerator. Provided it has kept cool the dish can be warmed-up a second time. Fungi are extremely good as salads but, as explained on p. 44, some species are not good to eat raw. So it is safer, before using them for a salad, to boil them first. They will still retain their flavour and, with the variety of different, possible dressings they are always good as a salad.

Fungi are always good with meat, either simply as a vegetable, or as stuffing, or in more sophisticated recipes. An otherwise quite dull soup can be completely transformed by adding a few, well-selected, fungi, or a little fungus powder or extract. Then again, too little is known of the possibility of using certain fungi for sweet dishes although some of them have quite a sweet perfume and positively invite this treatment. These can be baked into cakes, made into tarts, or be served like fruit, stewed with sugar. New discoveries of this kind are pleasant, as well as rewarding, and anyone who likes fungi should carry out a few experiments of his own.

Provided sound, undecayed specimens are found, it is not normally considered necessary to cut them in half to inspect for maggots. Any maggot holes will show, either on the surface, and at the bottom of the stem, if this is cut across. In doubtful cases, a piece of the cap can be broken off. Neither are any of the edible species normally considered sufficiently indigestible to make it necessary to slice them finely. Many recipes call for slicing, and this probably brings out the flavour, but many French and Italian recipes (as well as the pleasant English tradition of frying mushrooms—and many of the edible fungi are just as good—with the breakfast bacon) call for whole caps, grilled, fried, or baked. Translator's note.

MEDICINE FROM FUNGI

'There is nothing without poison. Only the dose determines whether a thing is poisonous.' In accordance with these words of the great Paracelsus many poisonous plants have to-day come to be used as valuable medicines. It was in this spirit that the poisonous fungi were considered, to see whether they could be used as medicines, and also as antidotes to their own poisons. Chemists have been trying to isolate the various poisons and to obtain them in a pure state chiefly in order to obtain a serum (e.g. anti-phalloidian serum) which would provide immunity and also, in serious cases, save lives. But many years of complicated experiments are still necessary to perfect this, requiring the use of a good many hundredweight of fresh poisonous fungi. Several bad fungus years can hold-up, or hinder this work.

Of the many Polypores which have been used as tinder, the most important is the *Fomes fomentarius*. This is a dangerous parasite, growing on Birch and causing white rot (in the United Kingdom it is believed to be confined to the Scottish Highlands). It can live up to 15 years. The cap is smokey-grey to black, hoof-shaped to semi-circular, flat underneath and growing on the tree without a stem, up to 32 cm. wide and 16 cm. high, the margin blunt and streaked with grey or tawny-red. The cortex is thick and tough, smooth and dull, with concentric grooves. The tubes are grey, later brown, rounded, and in several layers, the spores nearly spindle-shaped, 15–22μ long. The flesh is rust-brown and downy. This is the *'Fungus igrarius, Fungus chirurgorum, Agaricus chirurgorum'* of the early books on medicine. On the Continent it used to be greatly prized and was used, depending on its quality and the method of preparation, both as a dressing for wounds to stop bleeding, and as tinder to light fires. Remains of tinder fungus have been found, along with household utensils, in prehistoric pile-dwellings and both methods of use probably date back to the very earliest times.

One way of preparing it is to cut off the softest, downiest portions and to soften this further, either by stewing or soaking in hot water. It is then beaten with a mallet and rubbed until it is as soft as fine leather. It is then ready for use on wounds and, in parts of Germany, is still used in this way for minor cuts.

Tougher pieces of the fungus are soaked in a mixture of hot water, or urine, and ashes. They are then beaten soft and soaked again, in a solution of saltpetre, or salt, ashes, and saltpetre. These can then be used as tinder. They will light from a spark, and they go on glowing for a long time.

In ancient times this was often the only way in which primitive people could light a fire. Some very old people in country districts of Germany still use this method instead of the 'new-fangled invention', matches. As a matter of interest, it may be mentioned that, because of their leathery texture, these fungi have in the past been used to make hats or caps and other articles of clothing. In parts of Bavaria there was, until quite recently, a regular home industry using these fungi. This has only recently given way to the march of progress and has now died out.

Another polypore, too hard to use as a wound-dressing or as tinder, but useful for keeping a fire going, is the *Phellinus (= Polyporus) igniarius, Fomes*. This grows mostly on the trunks of poplar and willows. When young, the cap is rusty yellow-brown and almost globular, later blackish-brown and hoof- or bracket-shaped, up to 30 cm. wide and 10 cm. thick. The skin is smooth, greyish, with deep concentric zones and radial cracks. The 'flesh' is red-brown and hard as wood. The pores are grey, later cinnamon-brown, the tubes in layers, the spores transparent, rounded, 5–6μ long. It lives up to 30 years and does a good deal of harm to the trees on which it grows.

One of the oldest medicines made from fungi is probably that from the *Ungulina (= Polyporus) officinalis*. This fungus grows on the stems of larches in Southern Europe, Switzerland, Southern Russia, and Siberia. Its cap is tough, bracket- or hoof-shaped, very irregular, with concentric grooves and yellow and brown zones. The tubes are short and rather narrow, yellow-brown, not in layers. The flesh is whitish, tough though at first fairly soft, later woody but brittle, with a mealy smell and a taste which is at first sweetish and then decidedly bitter.

This fungus was known to the ancients and is mentioned by Galen, Dioscorides, and Pliny. It was prescribed by doctors and was also in popular use in the home both as a drastic purge and, used externally, as an effective way to stop bleeding. According to the ancient herbals it was also used successfully for chronic catarrh, diseases of the breast and lungs, as a remedy for night-sweating with tuberculosis, for rheumatism, gout, jaundice, dropsy, and intestinal worms. It contains resins and agaric acid which is effective in stopping perspiration, and it is used to-day in homoeopathic doses as '*Boletus laricis (Agaricus albus).*' This ancient remedy is also used to-day in various German 'digestive' liqueurs such as 'Heiligenbitter' and 'Alter Schwede.'

Many other species, mentioned as medicines by St. Hildegard, who died as Abbess of Bingen in the year 1180, can hardly be identified to-day. She may, among others, be referring to *Trametes suaveolens,* or to our notorious dry-rot fungus, *Merulius lacrimans.* One of her descriptions is fairly certainly our Jew's Ear, *Auricularia auricula*–the 'Fungus sambuci' of the old herbals. The Jew's Ear was frequently used medicinally, especially as a poultice for inflamed eyes, and as a gargle for inflammation of the throat. For this purpose it was either stewed in milk or softened in rose-water and used as an infusion. It does not seem to have been considered from the point of view of edibility, although it is edible and quite good. However, it seems to be somewhat indigestible and needs to be sliced for eating. In the Far East it is a delicacy and is regarded by the Chinese as a valuable article of trade. It contains the sugar: trehalose.

Very important in medicine, also to-day, is the parasitic ascomycete *Claviceps purpurea, Ergot*. It was known in ancient China, and was later used medicinally in Europe, especially since Lonitzer's herbal of 1582 where it is mentioned as 'Secale cornutum' or 'Fungus secalis'. It has been used to stop bleeding and, especially in child-birth, to assist the labour and arrest bleeding of the womb. On account of its dangerous side-effects its use to-day is very carefully supervised. To the botanist this fungus is an interesting example of the alternation of generations which takes place in three successive stages. The nearly-black, dark-violet sclerotium (permanent mycelium), white inside, grain-like, horn-shaped, hard and woody, which occurs on the inflorescences of rye and other grasses is intended to survive the Winter and, besides being rich in fat, contains the deadly poisons, Ergotine and Cornutine. When such infected rye has been ground and made into bread it has caused the terrible disease known as Ergotism. Outbreaks of this have occured in the past like mass epidemics, causing widespread suffering. The illness, which usually ends fatally, is very painful. There may be gangrene of the limbs, or serious nervous symptons with attacks of madness and considerable danger of suicide. Since it is now possible, with modern machinery, to purify the grain almost completely the disease has now become very rare. Only remote regions with backward agriculture and lack of supervision may still suffer from it. The last outbreak was in 1951, at Pont St. Esprit in the French Department of the Rhône. In recent times the poisons in this fungus have been thoroughly investigated. From them some extremely effective drugs have been produced which are more easily controlled than Ergot and which are very useful in gynaecology. They go under various trade names (Ergotamin, Gynergen) and are only obtainable on a doctor's prescription. They have recently been to some extent superceded by less dangerous German drugs.

The healing power of the yeasts was not unknown to the wine- and beer-brewers of Ancient Egypt and Babylon. Thus they were useful medicines even in those days. Yeast fungi are found whenever juices or liquids containing sugar are decomposed by alcoholic fermentation. They are single-cell, microscopically small fungi belonging to the ascomycetes. Among them are the wine-yeast: *Saccharomyces ellipsoideus,* and the beer-yeast, *Saccharomyces cerevisiae.* These are universally-known by-products in the manufacture of wine and beer and the yeast ferments must have been used for baking bread and cakes quite early in human history. With the fermentation of the sugar in the dough alcohol is formed, which soon escapes, and also carbonic acid. This tries to escape, producing bubbles in the dough, and making the bread or cake 'rise'. Leaven, which soon took the place of fresh yeast in making bread, contains innumerable yeast-fungi which ferment the dough and make it rise. Since various, vitally important substances—especially vitamins of the B group—have been found in yeast, this has been used successfully in the treatment of various deficiency- and skin-diseases. So the yeast-fungus, the smallest of our ascomycetes, is certain to endure. The entire distilling and fermentation industries are behind it to guarantee its future.

The gasteromycetes, especially the quite-ordinary Lycoperdon and Bovista species (the puff balls) have, among country people, for centuries had the reputation of being very effective medicines. For a long time these ideas were ridiculed and were believed only by shepherds, peasants, and gipsies. In earlier times these common fungi had quite an honoured place in homely medical books as *'Fungus bovista, Fungus rotundus, Bovista chirurgorum'* and *'Fungus chirurgorum'*. The olive-brown spore dust of these fungi was used for centuries, and is used to-day in country districts in Bavaria, as a healing powder for wounds, to arrest serious bleeding, especially for haemorrhoids, and also as a powder for children – with undoubted success. As reliable proof of their healing powers I will simply mention Kallenbach, who relates his own experience in the *Zeitschrift für Pilzforschung* (Mycological Journal), page 55, 1940. He describes how his own leg, which was thought to need amputation, was completely and quickly cured as a result of treatment with badgers' fat and the spore dust of the Bovista species. Old country people have told me of similar experiences.

The *Elaphomyces granulatus, cervinus* was used in earlier times as an aphrodisiac. In old fungus books it was described as *'Fungus cervinus, Boletus cervinus, Tubera cervina'*. It is a small to wallnut-sized ascomycete, globular, orange-yellow to brown, covered with small, grainy warts. It has a thick skin, is whitish to reddish inside and encloses a dark-brown to dark-violet mass of spores streaked by grey veins. It grows in late Autumn in coniferous woods, especially under pines, underground but near the surface. It has an unusual, very spicy smell and a bitter taste. It is inedible, but it is occasionally used by country people as a remedy for weakness, and is otherwise still used by peasants to stimulate cattle for breeding. Sometimes its presence in the surface-layer of the ground is indicated by little club-shaped fungi such as the *Cordyceps capitata Holmsk* or the tongue-shaped *Cordyceps ophioglossoides Ehr*.

The Fly Agaric, *Amanita muscaria* has been used therapeutically from the earliest times as a powder or tincture for swollen glands, serious swellings, nervous diseases, epilepsy and consumption. It is still used to-day in homoeopathic doses under the name *'Agaricus muscarius'*. For this, an essence is made from the fresh fungus. It is used, greatly diluted, for St. Vitus' Dance, heart ailments, rheumatoid arthritis, and scrofulous inflammation of the eye. (see p. 41).

The *Boletus satanus* contains the medically-effective agaric acid, phosphoric acid, resins, and fatty acids and is used in homoeopathic doses, very diluted, for dysentery as well as for diseases of the gallbladder and the liver. The *Lactarius piperatus* was used in ancient times, on account of its diuretic action, for kidney and bladder troubles as well as for stone or calculus.

The Stinkhorn, *Phallus impudicus* was already being used in 1619 for the treatment of gout. A certain Dr. Karo of Berlin is actually said to have cured skin cancer with it and to have had notable success in treating internal cancer, but this is noted for what it is worth. (See also p. 113).

Observers of Fairy Rings made by the larger fungi noticed that, while there was unusually rich growth at the periphery of these rings, there were other areas where the vegetation had died. Investigation of this showed that these fungi contained antibiotic, that is seed-killing, substances. Hollande first noticed this phenomenon with the large *Aspropaxillus candidus* (= Clitocybe candida), with the *Aspropaxillus giganteus* (= Clitocybe gigantea) and also with the *Clitocybe geotropa.* The active principle, which he called Clitocybin, has anti-tubercular properties and can kill the tubercular baccilli.

Swedish, French, and Russian scientists working in the 1940's isolated anti-biotics which can be used to combat disease-producing bacteria from the species Lactarius, from the *Calocybe Georgii* (= *Tricholoma gambosum*)-the St. George's Mushroom, from the *Clitocybe nebularis,* and from other of the larger fungi. These became known under the names, among others, of Laktaroviolin, Nebularin, Pleurotin, Polyporin, Biformin, and Irpexin. For some years, especially since the introduction of the 'wonder-drug' Penicillin, research has been concentrated on the ascomycetes, especially on moulds, and on the microscopically small ray fungi in the soil. Yet Penicillin, Streptomycin, Aureomycin and all the other anti-biotics are really the same as the curious 'dirt medicines' of the Middle Ages, transformed to spotless cleanliness by microbiological laboratories. If peasants in the old days, in Ireland and elsewhere, used to scrape the green mould off a piece of damp bread and use it to cure festering wounds, what is that in fact, except Penicillin treatment? The long-forgotten wisdom of the peasants, the teaching of that great doctor at the beginning of modern times, Theophrastus Bombastus of Hohenheim, who called himself Theophrastus and has been misrepresented as a charlatan, or for that matter, the wisdom of simple people like shepherds and farmers who lived close to nature-all this knowledge is merely being rediscovered to-day, cleared of its old-fashioned lumber, and delivered up to the modern witches' kitchen of the chemical industry!

The effects of Penicillin on bacteria, preventing their growth and also killing them, were discovered in 1928 by Alexander Fleming when he noticed that a bacteria culture had a 'dead zone' where a piece of mould had accidently formed. After patient work, the fungus was recognised as *Penicillium notatum* and Penicillin was isolated by an Oxford group under Florey and Chain.

Since the war, after earlier difficulties, Penicillin has been mass-produced with the help of American laboratories. Now it has become possible to manufacture it synthetically and, with a new method of culture discovered in 1949 by Lembke and developed by a firm in Hamburg, it is also mass-produced in Germany. Penicillin is especially effective for all kinds of infections and is used for abscesses, osteomyelitis, meningitis, and also for pneumonia, puerpural fever, peritonitis, venereal disease, tetanus, and gangrene. It is usually given as an injection, but also in the form of powder, ointment, and tablets.

Streptomycin was discovered in 1944 by the Americans, Waksman, Schatz, and Bugie in research on more than 10,000 fungus cultures from metabolism products of the ray fungus *Streptomyces* (formerly *Actinomyces) griseus.* This type of ray fungus comes from the throat of a sick hen! One is irresistibly reminded of Galen and his potent medicine from chicken-dung! Streptomycin is especially effective with certain forms of tuberculosis, especially tuberculosis of the brain in children, with typhus, and in many other cases where Penicillin fails, but also in combination with Penicillin.

Chloromycetin was discovered by Ehrlich and Joslyn in 1947 from *Streptomyces venezuelae* when examining 20,000 fungus cultures originating from 6,000 soil tests, and was in fact found in a field in Venezuela. It is now produced synthetically and is administered in the form of capsules for typhoid fever, paratyphoid, psittacosis, and other infections.

Terramycin was discovered by Finley in 1950 after long research into soil fungi and isolated from the ray fungus *Streptomyces rimosus.* It is administered in the form of capsules, drops, and injections and is effective in the treatment of whooping cough, pneumococcus, pneumonia and other infections diseases. Chemically it is very closely related to Aureomycin.

Aureomycin was discovered by Dugger in 1948 in the *Streptomyces aureofaciens,* which is also a ray fungus, when he was examining 3,400 fungus cultures. It is administered in capsules and is very effective in the treatment of many infectious diseases, including virus infections.

Tyrothricin was isolated in 1939 by Dubos from the *Bacillus brevis* found in marshy soil. It is marketed under the name Tyrosolvin and is effective in the treatment of many bacterial diseases.

Finally it should be mentioned that antibiotics made from ray fungi have recently become known which are said to have been effective in the treatment of certain forms of cancer. One awaits further development, especially in this field, with all reserve, but still with some hope that the lower fungi may yet furnish a weapon against this terrible scourge.

All these highly-effective, modern remedies derive from the lower ascomycetes, ray fungi, and bacteria and are microscopic flora from rubbish heaps, ponds, swamps, and so on. Quietly, slinking up the back stairs, a lot of ancient wisdom and medicine is coming back to us. We still smile unbelievingly, but we are already uncertain, and ready to be won over by the Ancients. However, now perhaps the larger fungi will have their turn. We learned from Moser in his

27

27. THE SHAGGY CAP, *Coprinus comatus* p 83

Edible

Edible

28. THE FAIRY RING CHAMPIGNON,
Marasmius oreades (upper) p 84
29. THE HORN OF PLENTY,

Caution

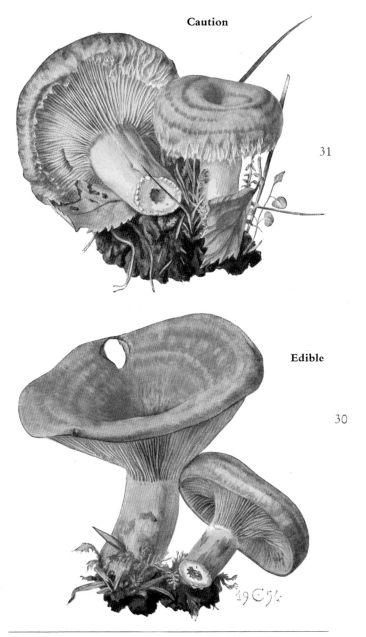

31

Edible

30

30. THE SAFFRON MILK CAP, *Lactarius deliciosus* (lower) p 85
31. THE WOOLLY MILK CAP, *Lactarius torminosus* (upper) p 86

32

19C'54

32. *Lactarius volemus* p 86

'Sydovia, Annales mycologici', 1951 that some fungi had already been found among the genus Cortinarius which had great antibiotic effect on typhoid bacteria, staphylococcic infections, as well as in other directions. However, in order to carry on further work in this direction a systematic classification of the genus is first essential. So, once again, the important of that often-ridiculed, and 'merely theoretical' science of systematic classification is proved to be of value.

CULTIVATION OF EDIBLE FUNGI

Many people have hoped to be able to pick the best of the edible fungi at any time, without the trouble of searching for them, and so there have been many attempts to cultivate the edible species. However, successful cultivation depends on a very great many factors which are as yet imperfectly understood. So cultivation has so far only been successful in the case of a few excellent gill-fungi mostly living on humus, dung, or timber.

The best results have so far been obtained with the Cultivated Mushroom. This is an agaric, probably descended from a white variety of the twin-spored Champignon, the *Agaricus bisporus*. This is found at roadsides and on manure heaps. It has a grey-brown cap with radial fibres and a whitish, incurved margin. The gills are fairly crowded, a pleasant pink when young, later chocolate brown. The white, smooth stem is evenly thick, fairly short and compressed. Before the cap is open the veil forms two thick swellings round the stem. This remains only as a thick, angular ring which can be pulled downwards. The white, soft, flesh colours slightly pink when fresh, and when bruised turns almost tawny-red. When fresh it smells of wood or of plums, has a mild taste, pleasantly nutty, and colours blood-red with aniline. The rounded spores are 7.5μ long and there are two spores on each basidium. It is an independant form of *Agaricus hortensis Cooke*.

In France the cultivation of mushrooms has been going on for centuries and is excellently organised in large, deep quarries and in the catacombs of Paris. The climate is there probably more favourable than in Germany. Nevertheless, before the war some 5,000 tons were being produced annually in Germany.[*]

The centre of mushroom cultivation in these days, however, is the United States where, especially in Pennsylvania, a highly-developed mushroom industry has been created. There they have succeeded in changing from cultivation on horse-manure to mass-cultivation on artificial sources of nourishment such as waste-products from industry. It seems unnecessary to describe the Cultivated Mushroom since it is so well known and can be seen everywhere in the shops.

---

[*] According to The Ministry of Agriculture 28,000 tons of cultivated mushrooms were grown in the U.K. in 1965. Translator's note.

E

Cultivation of the so-called micorrhiza-fungi – which can only flourish in close symbiosis with certain trees – among which are numbered most Boleti, as well as the Russulas and the Chanterelle has, for obvious reasons, not been successful until now. However the *Pleurotus ostreatus* (The Oyster Mushroom),* the *Flammulina velutipes*, and the *Pholiota (Kuehneromyces) mutabilis* as well as others which grow on the stumps of deciduous trees can be cultivated by grafting and other methods of planting the spores. Since Molisch and Mayr brought over the *Shiitake* fungus from East Asia where it is universally cultivated, the cultivation of this excellent fungus has been tried several times with success in Germany.

By taking into account their own type of natural habitat a good many other fungi can be replanted, including the Morels and various Helvellas. Ink Caps can be grown on rubbish- and compost-heaps and *Tricholoma nudum* and *Clitocybe nebularis* can be grown on sweepings from deciduous woods. On woodland paths and clearings it is possible to grow the *Calocybe Georgii*, *Clitopilus prunulus*, *Paxillus involutus*, *Lepiota procera* (The Parasol Mushroom), *Leucoagaricus excoriatus*, *Laccaria laccata* and others. Probably the *Nematoloma capnoides*, the *Polyporus giganteus*, the *Polyporus squamosus*, the *Marasmius oreades* and the *Sparassis crispa*, as well as several others, will also flourish if transplanted. Here is a wide-open field for energetic fungus lovers.

---

* The Oyster Mushroom, so-called from its shape which is not unlike an oyster-shell is, when young, a good, edible fungus. It is found on stumps and fallen or dying trunks of elm and beech throughout the year, but especially in late Autumn and Winter. The cap is flattened, shell-shaped, deep blue-grey to black when young, brown when old. The stem is short and white and appears to grow out of the side of the cap. The gills are white, decurrent. The spores are pale lilac. This fungus often grows in clusters. Translator's note.

DESCRIPTIONS

(In the following descriptions edible and poisonous species are so marked. 'Caution' means that, as described in the text, the species may be dangerous and care is needed.

Spore dimensions are measured in thousandths of a millimetre. One thousandth of a millimetre is known as a micron and is represented by the Greek letter µ. Thus, say, 9µ means 9/1,000 mm.).

1. THE DEATH CAP

Amanita phalloides

Poisonous

Plate 1, facing p. 26 (left)

When this fungus first appears above ground it appears to be covered with a white, egg-shaped membrane—the universal veil. When this tears the cap is pale-green, globular to bell-shaped, then convex to CAP flattened, 5–15 cm. (exceptionally 20 cm.) in diameter. The colour is then typically olive to grey-green, streaked with radiating dark fibrils and, occasionally, with patches of the veil remaining on the cap as white flakes or warts. The gills remain white and are soft, unequal in GILLS length, wide, very close-set, and narrowing to free. The spore dust is SPORES white. The spores are transparent, globular to egg-shaped, 8–10µ long, staining blue in iodine. The slender stem, up to 12 cm. long, is STEM white or yellowish, sometimes with greenish streaks and with a similarly-coloured, downward-hanging ring. (The ring is at first a RING membrane stretching from the margin of the cap to the stem. This tears as the fungus grows, leaving traces of the imprint of the gills still showing on the ring.) The stem is at first solid but soon becomes hollow from the top downwards. The base is thick and bulbous, well set in the ground, and covered with a whitish, thick-skinned, ragged membranous sheath or volva. The flesh is white and soft, sometimes VOLVA with greenish-yellow streaks under the skin of the cap, and has a mild taste. The characteristic, honey-sweet smell is at first slight, becoming increasingly stronger and finally obtrusive and objectionable. (If a potato-like smell is noticed the fungus is probably the yellow *Amanita citrina*—2 below).

The Death Cap is common from late Summer to Autumn in woods, gardens, and pastures, especially under oak trees. It grows singly or in groups and is deadly poisonous even in small quantities.

A less-common, white variety is the *Amanita verna* (The Fool's Mushroom) which appears as early as May. This has a compressed ring and a more slender base and sheath. It is also deadly poisonous and even contact (i.e. with the spores) may sometimes be dangerous.

Similarly-coloured fungi such as the green Russulas or Tricholomas have no ring. The *Tricholoma flavovirens* (10) has yellow gills and
yellow flesh. With the Russulas, and especially the edible *Russula
Heterophylla,* confusion can occur if they are cut and not lifted from
the ground with the base intact since the most important characteristic
is then missing. Even then, the firm, brittle flesh and gills, which are
typical, reveal that they are Russulas. The Death Cap can also be mistaken for one of the varieties of the common mushroom – the Psal-
liotas. However none of these when mature have white gills, the
colours varying from pink to light chocolate or dark brown, nor is
their spore dust ever white like that of the Amanitas. Confusion with
puff-balls when they are young and egg-shaped is also possible, but
these can be recognised at once by cutting them longtitudinally.
Fungi which are too young to reveal distinguishing features are, in
any case, better ungathered.

Most cases of serious fungus poisoning are due to the Amanitas and
beginners would be well advised to avoid these entirely, or to eat only
those which have been identified with certainty by an expert. They
are the more dangerous to the careless because they look attractive,
do not smell at all unpleasantly when they are young, and have a by-
no-means unpleasant taste.

The symptons of poisoning do not show immediately. It is only
after 10–12 hours – dangerously late for effective treatment – that severe
abdominal pains, vomitting, and diarrhoea, together with extreme
thirst, are felt. If, therefore, discomfort is felt several hours after eating
fungi, there is considerable danger and a doctor should be called at
once. For details of the various symptons of poisoning, see **page 39.**

2. DESTROYING ANGEL

Amanita Virosa

Poisonous

Plate 2, facing p. 26 (right)

The white *Amanita virosa* is also covered with a universal veil and is
egg-shaped when it first shows above ground. Its small to medium-
sized cap is sharply conical, the edge frequently inturned, then bell-
shaped, and only rarely completely expanded, 3–7 (12) cm. wide. It
is sticky in wet weather, with a silky sheen in dry. The centre of the
cap is ivory-coloured, later tinged tawny-red, sometimes with patches
of the veil remaining on the cap or at the edges. The cap peels. The
gills are pure white, soft, narrow, unequal in length, almost distant
and free, woolly when cut. The spore dust is white, the spores
transparent, egg-shaped conical, 7–10 (12)µ long, and stain blue in
iodine. The stem is of even thickness, slender, up to 15 cm. long, with
white fibres or scales, stuffed to hollow, with a thin, white, ragged,

CAP

GILLS
SPORES

STEM

woolly, hanging transient, grooved ring. The base is round and
bulbous, covered with a large white skinny, often clinging, volva   VOLVA
usually fairly deep in the ground. The flesh is white, soft, at first with
a slightly sweet smell, soon becoming musty and finally nauseous.
The taste is mild, almost radish-like, and the flesh stains bright yellow
with caustic soda.

It occurs on mossy ground, especially under firs, in mixed woods
under beeches, from midsummer to late Autumn, mostly singly or in
scattered groups, in places in profusion. It is deadly poisonous.

Beginners may confuse it with the Common Mushroom with
which it does often occur. It is dangerously similar to the Horse Mushroom, *Agaricus (Psalliota) arvensis* (24) but this differs from the *Amanita
virosa* in the absence of a bulbous base with volva, by the typical
greyish-pink to dark chocolate-brown gills, by the gradual yellowing
of the bruised flesh, by its pleasant aniseed-like smell, as well as by the
chocolate brown spore dust.

The yellow-green *Amanita citrina, mappa*–the False Death Cap–
often resembles the *Amanita virosa*. The *Amanita citrina, mappa* has a
medium-large cap, 5–10 cm. wide, pale lemon-yellow, sometimes   CAP
almost white, or with a yellow-green shimmer, hemispherical to
expanded, always sticky and shining, covered with easily-removed,
felt-like remnants of the veil, either of the same colour as the cap or   VEIL
changing to brown. The gills are whitish and almost free. The spore   GILLS
dust is white, the individual spores transparent, spherical 7–10μ long,   SPORES
staining blue in iodine. The 8–10 cm. long, slender stem is the same   STEM
colour as the cap with a feltlike, whitish or yellowish downward-
hanging ring, and at the ground a well-defined, spherical bulbous end   RING
with attached, cup-like volva. The flesh is white and soft, with a sharp
musty smell resembling raw potatoes and a taste resembling turnips.   RING
It occurs from July to November, especially in conifer woods, less
frequently in deciduous woods. Its poison, Mappin, is, according to
Th. Wieland, identical with the Bufotenin secreted by toads. Although
itself comparatively harmless, this fungus should on no account be
eaten because of the possibility of confusion with the poisonous
Amanitas.

Somewhat similar is the *Amanita gemmata, junquillea*. This has a
waxy-yellow, or lemon to egg-yolk yellow cap and becomes paler   CAP
with age. It is 3–10 cm. wide, with fine grooves, white gills, a fairly   GILLS
slender white stem with a very fugitive, and therefore often no longer   STEM
recognisable, ring. It is without a bulbous base but has a thick, sheath-   RING
like, seperable volva. The spore dust is white, the single spores broadly-   VOLVA
elliptical, 10–12μ long. It is without taste or smell, probably hardly
poisonous, but should be avoided by beginners on account of possible
confusion–which can be deadly–with the poisonous Amanitas. (See
Poisoning, p. 39).

3. AMANITA PANTHERINA

Poisonous
Plate 3, facing p. 27 (right)

CAP   The cap of this medium-sized fungus is pale- to grey-brown or
dark brown, becoming paler with age. It is hemispherical, domed,
and soon expanded, 3–10 (12) cm. wide, with small, fairly-evenly
VEIL   distributed, pure-white, flaky remains of the veil. The cap has a
finely-grooved edge, peels easily, and is often clammy and slimy. The
GILLS   gills remain pure white, are free and close-set, narrowing towards
the stem, and are thick and hairy in cross section. The spore dust is
SPORES   white, the spores transparent, broadly-oval, granular, 8–12μ long.
STEM   They do not stain blue with iodine. The stem is slender, white,
membranous to flaky, stuffed, soon becoming hollow and has a white,
tattered, broad, steeply-downhanging ring without grooves. The
base of the stem is bulbous and globular with a clearly-differentiated,
VOLVA   bulging volva into which it seems to have been pushed, and above,
one or two belt-like rings. The flesh has a musty smell and a taste
like radishes. It stains wine-red in carbolic acid solution.

    It grows mostly singly in Summer and Autumn in deciduous and
pinewoods, or in grass near firs, rather closely resembles the *Amanita
spissa* (4) and, since it is poisonous, its resemblance to this edible
fungus is dangerous to all except experts. The comparison is shown
in the diagram below which clearly shows the distinguishing
features.

    Amateurs would be well-advised to avoid all Amanitas, including
the *Amanita rubescens* (6), of which the brown specimens can very

Left, the poisonous *Amanita pantherina*. Right, the *Amanita spissa*

closely resemble the *Amanita pantherina*. Any confusion here can be matter of life and death. (See the chapter 'Fungus Poisoning', p. 37).

4. AMANITA SPISSA

Caution

Plate 4, facing p. 27 (left)

The cap of this impressive, medium-sized fungus is 5–15 cm. in CAP
diameter, hemispherical to more-or-less flattened. Its colour is very
variable–silver-grey to grey-brown, with grey permanent remains
of the veil clinging to it. The edges are not striated. The white gills VEIL
are soft, crowded, broad, slightly-decurrent at the stem and woolly in GILLS
section. The spore dust is white, the spores egg-shaped, granular in SPORES
texture, 8–10μ long, staining blue with iodine. The sturdy stem is STEM
white or grey-white becoming grey, with a high-placed, white,
downward-hanging ring, always striated, and grey underneath. The RING
base of the stem is a firm, stumpy bulb covered with wartlike ex-
crescences and without a volva. The flesh is whitish, often with brownish streaks, greyish under the skin of the cap at the crown, with a mild
turnip or radish-like smell, and a mild taste reminiscent of turnips
when raw. It dyes purple in sulphuric acid.

This fungus appears early in the season, sometimes from May,
more frequently from June to October, growing mostly singly, not
infrequently in deciduous woods and especially in conifer woods,
sometimes near to the *Amanita pantherina* (3) with which it can easily
be confused.

It is an excellent edible fungus, but only to be recommended to
experts. Beginners should avoid it until they are quite sure of distinguishing it from the poisonous *Amanita pantherina*. Confusion here
can be a matter of life and death. (See diagram p 64, showing the
two together). The very similar brown forms of the *Amanita muscaria*
var. *umbrina* have, like the typical red variety, yellow-toned flesh
under the skin of the cap. The often very similar *Amanita rubescens* (6)
also has a striated ring and its flesh invariably reddens. Fungi which
are too young to show the typical characteristics should be avoided.

5. FLY AGARIC

Amanita muscaria

French: TUE-MOUCHE.
Italian: OVOLACCIO.
Spanish: AGARICO MATAMOSCAS.   **Poisonous**
German: FLIEGENPILZ.   Plate 5, facing p. 34 (left)

In the woods this beautiful and often very large fungus appears
above ground enclosed in its universal veil. The cap soon becomes CAP

hemispherical to flattened, brilliant scarlet or orange red with typical white or yellow warty remains of the veil which are easily rubbed-off when wet. At the edge of a wood it is often paler. The skin peels

GILLS easily. The gills remain pure white, thick and crowded, almost free at the stem, and are wooly in section. The spore-dust is white, the

SPORES spores broadly egg-shaped, 9–11μ long, and do not stain blue with

STEM iodine. The slender, robust stem, up to 25 cm. high is white, tapered towards the top, at first solid or stuffed, later hollow, with a whitish,

RING sturdy, downward-hanging, striated ring and ends in a thick, bulbous base with several rings of whitish, warty scales. The flesh is white and soft, lemon yellow under the skin of the cap, with hardly any smell, a mild taste, and stains wine-red with carbolic acid. Even quite young specimens may easily be recognised when cut by the lemon-yellow colouring under the skin. Lemon-yellow and yellow-brown varieties also occur *(Amanita regalis, umbrina, formosa.*

The bulbous base of the Fly Agaric, *Amanita muscaria*

It is common from June to October in conifer and deciduous woods, often in large numbers, and frequently near the *Boletus edulis.* When it first shows above ground it often resembles a white egg. It is covered with thick, often unbroken, friable warts and there is no sign of the colour which

it later acquires. Soon however, the veil tears into numerous flakes, easily washed away by rain, with patches of orange or blood red showing between them. Within one or two days the fungus grows considerably and opens-up, first bell-shaped, but soon wide open and brilliant in fine scarlet.

It is dangerous, and not only to flies against which it used to be broken-up and left to stand in milk or sugar-water. Muscarine is only one of the poisons present in this fungus, probably not even the most important, and mostly present in the skin of the cap. It is not destroyed by cooking, is very soluble in water, and may perhaps be removed in the cooking water. However much the edibility of this fungus may be disputed, it is undoubtedly dangerous and may occasionally cause death. The poison acts on the nerves, can cause severe hallucinations, a form of intoxication, and other symptoms. It is used in medicine, see p 41.

6. THE BLUSHER
Amanita rubescens

Caution

French: GOLMOTE, ORONGE VINÉUSE   Plate 6, facing p. 34 (right)

CAP The cap is hemispherical to flattened, 5–15 cm. in diameter, and varies in appearance from small and delicate to large and sturdy.

Edible

33

33. *Lactarius piperatus* p 87

Edible

35

Edible

34

19 C 54

34. *Russula cyanoxantha* (lower) p 88
35. *Russula vesca* (upper) p 88

36

37

36. *Russula fellea* (upper) p 89
37. *Russula ochroleuca* (lower) p 90

Edible

38

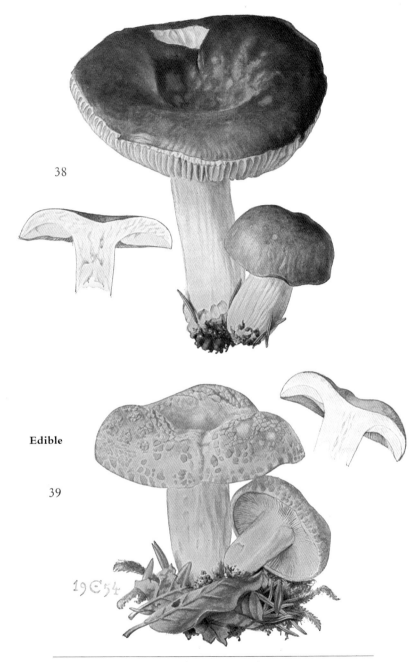

Edible

39

19E54

38. *Russula integra* (upper) p 90
39. *Russula virescens* (lower) p 91

40

40. THE SICKENER, *Russula emetica* p 92

Edible

41. *Hygrophorus (Camarophyllus) pratensis* p 93

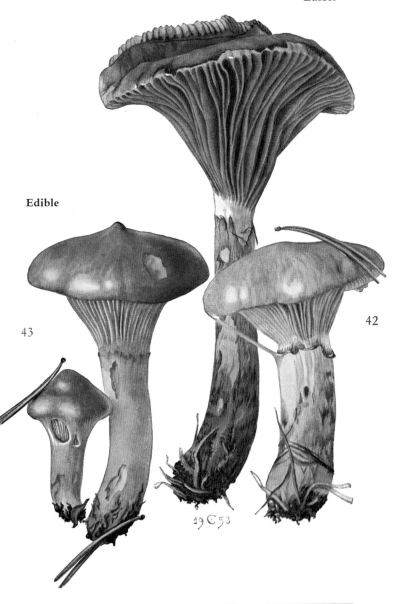

Edible

Edible

43

42

42. *Gomphidius glutinosus* (right) p 93
43. *Gomphidius rutilus (viscidus)* (left) p 94

Edible

44

Edible

45

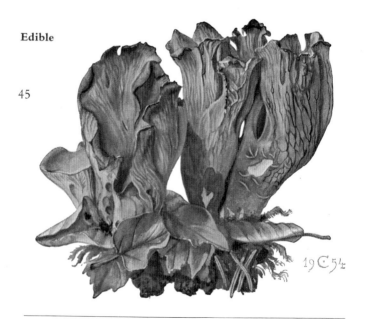

19C54

---

44. THE CHANTERELLE, *Cantharellus cibarius* (upper) p 95
45. *Gomphus clavatus* (lower) p 95

It is pink, or almost-white to flesh-coloured, or copper-red to a variety of shades of brown and finally, when old, a shade of violet. The pale, never pure white, mostly rather flat, warty remains of the veil are at first thickly distributed over the cap but are easily rubbed off, and after heavy rain are washed off so that the cap is bald. The skin peels easily. The gills, attached to the stem by a slight tooth, are unequal in length, white, often reddish. The spore dust is white, the spores egg-shaped, granulated, 8–9µ long, staining blue with iodine. The stem is more-or-less pinkish or flesh-coloured, solid when young, later hollow, slender and sturdy. It is up to 15 cm. high and has a large, white or yellow to grey-violet, hanging, tough, and always noticeably-striated, ring. Towards the base the stem is thickened and gradually terminates, without a clearly-marked transition, in a scaly, or sometimes smooth, bulb without a volva. The flesh is white (pink or flesh-coloured under the top of the cap) and, if broken or damaged by animals, slowly reddens on exposure to the air, especially at the base of the stem and in maggot-holes. Much as this fungus otherwise varies, this colour change is its most distinguishable characteristic. The flesh quickly stains wine-red in carbolic acid. The smell is pleasant, the taste mild but with acrid overtones. The Blusher is poisonous when raw but easily digestible, edible and excellent cooked. It is best cleaned by peeling. It is not suited to drying.

VEIL

GILLS

SPORES

STEM

RING

The fungus is common in deciduous and conifer woods, appearing very early, from the beginning of Summer, to late Autumn, mostly singly, but widely distributed and occasionally plentifully.

There are a number of varieties depending on habitat. Worth noting is the *Amanita pseudorubescens*, a doubtful, alleged poisonous, variety. The cap is said to be dark violet-brown with pointed warty flakes on the cap, a grey-violet stem and similarly-coloured ring. Beginners should be careful to avoid confusion with the poisonous *Amanita pantherina* (3) and with the brown forms of Amanita. Also young specimens, in which the characteristics are not clearly marked, should be avoided. In any case, all Amanitas are more-or-less poisonous when raw.

7. THE GRISETTE

Amanita (Amanitopsis) vaginata

Caution

French: AMANITE ENGAINEE   Plate 7, between pp 34 and 35

The cap is 4–12 cm. in diameter, at first egg-shaped, and completely or partly enveloped by the universal veil. It soon becomes bell-shaped to convex and finally flattened, often umbonate★, with marked

CAP

★ Umbonate–with a central swelling like the boss of a shield.

striations extending from the margin to one third the diameter of the cap, lead-grey to whitish grey, sometimes covered with loose, filamentous or warty, grey-white remnants of the veil, but soon becoming free from these. The flesh is thin and the skin is difficult to **GILLS** peel without damaging the flesh beneath. The gills are white, free, **SPORES** fairly crowded. The spore dust is white, the spores white, globular, **STEM** granulated, 9–12μ long. The stem is white to greyish, 10 cm. or more high, without a ring. It tapers towards the top, is at first solid, then tubular, hollow, with flaky remains of the veil, and very fragile. The base is not bulbous and is surrounded by a large, thick, whitish sheath as though enclosed in a bag. The flesh is white, very fragile, with no smell and a mild taste.

The complete veil (left) and the base of the stem (right) of the Grisette – *Amanita (Amanitopsis) vaginata*

This fungus is common in deciduous and conifer woods from May-June to October. It is poisonous when raw but edible and well-flavoured when cooked. Since it is so fragile it is best kept separate from larger fungi. You can almost see it grow since it needs only warm, damp weather to emerge and develop.

The white, orange-coloured, and red-brown forms are to-day considered as different varieties with their own names: *Amanita nivalis, Amanita crocea, Amanita fulva*. These are also edible. Very young specimens, especially the white forms, should be avoided by beginners at all costs in view of the danger of confusion with the Death Cap. The tall stem, without a ring or bulbous base, surrounded by the large, ragged sheath or volva, the marginally deeply-striated cap, and its fragility are characteristic enough to distinguish it from the poisonous Amanitas. Its white spores easily distinguish it from the red-spored Volvaria species.

8. THE PARASOL MUSHROOM

Lepiota procera

French: COULEMELLE ELEVEE.
Italian: BUBBOLA MAGGIORE.
Spanish: SETA DE ANILLO.   **Edible**
German: RIESENSCHIRMLING.   Plate 8, between pp 34 and 35

The cap of this easily-recognised, always impressive, fungus is   CAP
first hemispherical to egg-shaped and closed by a double-layered
white flaky ring between the cap and the stem. The cap is later bell-
shaped and, when expanded, parasol- or plate-shaped. It is 8–25 (30)
cm. in diameter, sometimes considerably more, with a stumpy, dark-
brown boss, or umbo. The leathery skin is dull white to brown with
large, shaggy, tufted brown scales. The skin cannot be peeled without
tearing the flesh underneath. The gills are white, free, crowded,   GILLS
broad and soft. The spores are elliptical, granular, 12–18 (20)μ long.   SPORES
The spore dust is white. The very slender, 15–30 cm. high, cylindrical
stem, easily detached from the cap, is coarsely fibrous, streaked with   STEM
brown and, though easily broken, is almost woody with its long
fibres. It is hollow, smooth at the top, with an upwards–standing,   STEM
robust, readily moveable double ring, and is thickened to a felty bulb
at the base. The flesh of the cap is invariably white and very soft. The
smell is earthy and not unpleasant, the taste pleasant and nutty.   RING

Young Parasol Mushrooms are excellent to eat, older specimens are
leathery and the stems woody and tough. Unbroken large specimens
are very good, dipped in egg-and-breadcrumbs and cooked like a

The early stage of the
Parasol Mushroom with
cap closed and the future
ring

Wiener Schnitzel. Older, tougher specimens, sliced and dried, are very good as
flavouring.

The Parasol Mushroom occurs fairly
frequently, singly and in clusters, from
July to October, especially near the edges
of woods, in cuttings and open spaces in
woods, also in grassy fields and pastures,
and even in gardens, especially near
ant-heaps. It is one of the largest fungi
and plate-size specimens do occur.

The earliest, disc-like form of the
Parasol is characteristic, and more so its
second, early stage when it resembles a
drum-stick, with an egg-shaped, closed
cap and fairly tough skin with brown
scales. The figure shows the closed cap
and embryo ring.

The Shaggy Parasol, *Lepiota rhacodes* is

found in similar habitats, especially on the edges of woods and woodland paths. It is very similar to the Parasol but smaller and more sturdy
in appearance. Its cap is grey-brown and the skin becomes broken up
into jagged, filamentous, concentric, shaggy scales. The spores are
smaller, 9–12μ long and elliptic. The stem is shorter, stouter, white
to reddish-brown, smooth or silky-fibred, bulbous at the base, with
a moveable firm ring. The flesh is white, becoming slowly saffron-
coloured when broken, with a pleasant smell and mild taste. It is
edible and, when young, extremely good, especially fried or grilled.

9. St. GEORGE'S MUSHROOM

Tricholoma gambosum

Italian : PRUGNOLO	**Edible**
German : MAIPILZ	Plate 9, between pp 34 and 35

CAP   The cap is medium-large, fleshy, hemispherical to domed with inturned edges, finally flattened and often wavy, ivory or cream-
white, dry with a dull matt surface, 5–10 (15) cm. in diameter. The
GILLS   gills are crowded, sinuate, pale white to creamy yellow, and brittle.
SPORES   The spore dust is white, the spores elliptical and fairly small, 4–6μ
STEM   long. The stem is short and thick, 4–8 cm. long, white to meal-
coloured, slightly fibrous and woolly with a fibrous skin. It is often
thickened and woolly at the base. The flesh is thick, soft, and whitish,
smelling strongly of meal or gherkins, and with a mild taste. This
fungus may appear before the end of April (by St. George's Day,
hence the name) up to the middle of June, seldom later.

It frequently grows at the edges of woods or in woodland ridges
and clearings, in parks under bushes, more rarely among conifers,
also frequently on moors and downs, sometimes in long rows, rings
or semi-circles. It is edible and very good. It is sometimes confused
with the deadly poisonous *Inocybe patouillardii* (19) which grows in the
same habitats, often resembles the St. George's Mushroom, and is at
first pure white but soon becomes reddish-brown and fibrous. Later
the caps of the *Inocybe patouillardii* are brownish. Its flesh colours
where touched and, if kept for 24 hours, becomes brick red. It also
has a different, pungent-fruity smell. Confusion with the poisonous
Rhodophyllus lividus (23) is also dangerous. Its white flesh also has a
mealy smell at first, but soon has a rancid, highly-unpleasant smell,
as also the extremely poisonous *Clitocybe dealbata* which has a white
cap but almost transverse gills.

10. TRICHOLOMA FLAVOVIRENS (EQUESTRE)

Edible

German: GRÜNLING   Plate 10, between pp 34 and 35 (upper)

The cap of this rather sturdy, fleshy fungus is no more than medium-   CAP
size,4–8 (10) cm., at first hemispherical to domed, than flat to
funnel-shaped, wavy, woolly-filamentous, inturned, olive- to
greenish-yellow, sometimes with a broad, olive-brown to tawny
umbo and sticky skin which peels easily. The gills are bright sulphur-   GILLS
yellow, broad, crowded, sinuate to free. The spore dust is white, the
spores transparent, egg-shaped, smooth, 5–8µ long. The stem is   SPORES
fairly short, full, 4–6 (10) cm. high, smooth, toned sulphur-yellow to   STEM
brown-green, bulbously-thickened at the base and deep-set in the
ground. The flesh is whitish to yellowish, lemon-yellow under the
skin of the cap. The smell and taste are slightly mealy, the taste
almost gherkin-like, mild and pleasant.

This fungus grows in sandy pinewoods from August to November
and is edible and good.

The somewhat similar *Tricholoma sulphureum* with pale, ochre-
tinged cap, white, almost-free, wide and distant gills, a white stem,
yellowish at the base with reddish-flecked scales, and flesh which is
sulphur-yellow when broken has a thoroughly unpleasant smell
rather like coal gas and a highly unpleasant taste. Similar, but paler,
is the *Tricholoma inamoenum*. This also smells of gas, has a thoroughly
unpleasant taste, and like the former, is probably poisonous. Yellow-
green forms of the variously-coloured *Tricholoma saponaceum* are
differentiated by their marked soapy smell, are probably not poisonous, but of little value and may cause discomfort if eaten. However,
the *Tricholoma flavovirens* could even be confused with the Death Cap.

11. THE WOOD BLEWIT

Tricholoma, (Lepista) nudum

French: LE MOUSSERON VRAI   **Edible**
German: NACKTER RITTERLING Plate 11, between pp 34 and 35 (lower)

The cap of this fungus is 6–12 (15) cm. in diameter, at first hemi-   CAP
spherical, smooth, violet to brownish-violet, often becoming paler.
The gills are crowded, thin, violet to brownish-lilac. The spore-dust   GILLS
is whitish to slightly pinkish, the single spores greyish-red, egg-   SPORES
shaped, 6–8µ long. The stem is mostly short and full, fibrillose   STEM
towards the apex, often bulbous towards the base, and the same
colour as the cap. The violet flesh has an aromatic smell and a sour-
sweet taste.

The Wood Blewit appears in late Autumn (October to November). It is common in woods, especially in beechwoods, among dead leaves and compost, and grows in large clusters and Fairy Rings. It is a good edible fungus and well-suited to pickling in vinegar.

Very similar, although a paler blue to grey-violet is the *Lepista glaucocana* = *Tricholoma glaucocanum*, the cap and spore dimensions of which are very similar to the Wood Blewit, though it is rather more curved, or humped, and its smell mealy. It grows in pinewoods and is very good to eat.

Both the above are very similar to the Blewit, *Tricholoma (Lepista) saevum, (personatum)*. The cap is the same size and the spores are barely distinguishable from those of the above. Cap and gills are violet and the stem short and sturdy, violet to lilac. This fungus, which can survive frost, is found in meadows and among bushes, less frequently among pines, and occasionally in deciduous woods. It is edible and excellent to eat.

12. TRICHOLOMA PARDINUM (TIGRINUM)

Caution

Plate 12, between pp 34 and 35 (lower)

CAP   This is a medium-sized fungus. The cap is 6–10 (15) cm. wide, rounded-cone to bell-shaped, finally flattened to downturned, at first with completely inrolled, thin edges and a dry surface, violet- to silver-grey, turning brown when bruised, with large, grey-brown to ash-grey, or blackish, filamentous tile-like scales, rather paler at the

GILLS   margin. The gills are dull-white with yellow-green tones, wide and
SPORES   thick, curved, nearly free. The spores are whitish, egg-shaped, 8–10μ
STEM   long. The stem is whitish to pale-grey, sometimes brownish, sturdy, bulbous and filamentous. The apex of the stem shows drops of water when cut. The flesh is whitish, but grey to some depth under the skin of the cap, ochre-yellow or rust-coloured in the stem, smells strongly of fresh meal, and has a mild, slightly-mealy taste.

It occurs in Summer and Autumn on chalky ground among beeches and firs. Though poisonous it is not deadly and the taste is dangerously pleasant. It can cause serious intestinal and gastric troubles with sickness and diarrhoea, and long-lasting after effects. (See 'Fungus Poisoning', p 37).

The *Tricholoma pardinum* can be confused with the edible *Tricholoma terreum* (13). Plates 12 and 13, between pp 34, 35, show the two together with the edible and harmless *Tricholoma terreum* above. This is smaller and more delicate, little more than 6 cm. in diameter, and has no mealy smell. The gills are grey towards the margin of the cap and notched in section; the stem is hollow, fibrous, and greyish. The similar *Tricholoma scalpturatum (argyraceum)* has a slightly mealy smell and its gills are yellowish. Its grey cap has fine scales and is humped to flat, its stem fibrous and white with a grey, almost ring-shaped veil which is very transient. The spores are only 5–6μ in diameter. This fungus should be treated with caution.

13. TRICHOLOMA TERREUM

French: PETIT GRIS **Edible**
German: ERDRITTERLING Plate 13, between pp 34 and 35 (upper)

This small to medium-size fungus has a thin cap, 4–8 (10) cm. wide,   CAP
at first conical to egg-shaped, later flattened, but often with a pronounced umbo and wavy margin. The skin of the cap is mouse- or
brownish-grey to earth-coloured, scaly, often with rust-coloured
fibrils. The gills are free, notched, whitish, grey towards the margin,   GILLS
indented in section. The spore dust is white, the spores white,   SPORES
elliptical, 5–6μ long. The stem is slender, 3–8 (10) cm. high, at first   STEM
solid, later hollow, of even thickness, fragile, pale to greyish-white,
mealy at the apex, often reddish- or blue-green toned at the base. The
flesh is white or greyish like the cap, without smell or with a barely
perceptible mealy smell and a mild taste.

It is good to eat and appears from midsummer to late Autumn in
deciduous and conifer woods, especially under birches, at the edges
of woods and paths, among bushes and on sandy heaths, often in
clusters, and in places in large quantities.

Confusion with the poisonous *Tricholoma pardinum* (12) can be
dangerous, but this is more sturdy, with broad scales, darker gills,
and with a marked mealy smell. The inexperienced should avoid all
grey Tricholomas.

14. CLITOCYBE NEBULARIS

French: NÉBULEUX **Edible**
German: NEBELKAPPE Plate 14, between pp 34 and 35

The cap of this medium-sized fungus is fairly regular, though some-   CAP
times wavy, 6–12 (15) cm. in diameter, convex, finally flattened,
often umbonate, pale- or ash-grey to brownish-grey, darker in wet
weather, with a bloom easily rubbed off, later smooth. The skin peels
easily. The gills are whitish to ochre-yellow, thick, narrow, curved   GILLS
and decurrent, easily separated from the flesh of the cap (characteristic). The spores are white, egg-shaped, 6–8μ long. The stem is   SPORES
whitish to brownish, 6–10 cm. high, full and firm, later spongy, with   STEM
netlike fibrils and a bulbous base striated with white fibrils. The flesh
is fairly thick and firm, later soft, white with a pronounced, characteristic, almost unpleasant mealy smell and an acid, acrid taste.

It occurs from the end of September to November, growing in woods, bushes, and on heaths, often in large quantities. It is edible but not to everybody's taste and may cause considerable discomfort if eaten in large quantities. Only young specimens should be gathered, first simmered, and the cooking water discarded.

The *Clitocybe nebularis* can hardly be confused with any other species. The only other slightly similar fungus is the poisonous *Rhodophyllus lividus* (23) with an ivory-white to brownish-yellow, larer grey-brown cap. Its pale-yellow gills are fairly distant, sinuate, and become reddish with age.

15. THE HONEY FUNGUS

Armillaria mellea

Edible

German: HALLIMASCH   Plate 15, between pp 34 and 35

CAP   The Honey Fungus grows in clusters. The cap is at first spherical and completely closed, with a veil from the margin to the stem, then rounded to expanded, finally flattened to depressed, 3–12 (18) cm. in diameter. It is thin-fleshed, very varied in colour, honey-yellow to dull brown or tawny, striated at the margin and with rough, darker,
GILLS   easily rubbed-off flakes or scales in the central portion. The gills are fairly distant, adnate or sometimes decurrent, at first dirty-white, then reddish to brownish, often brown-streaked. The caps of the lower fungi in a cluster are often sprinkled with flour-like spore dust from
SPORES those growing above. The spore dust is white, the single spores
STEM   white, egg-shaped, granular and 7–9μ long. The stem is 5–12 (15) cm. high, solid, pale flesh-coloured at the apex, elsewhere yellow-brown and striated, when young with a yellowish bulbous base, later greenish-grey becoming blackish with coarse almost woody fibres,
RING   and with a yellow-white, upstanding, thick-skinned, tufted ring. The flesh is fairly thin, whitish to light brown, almost without smell. Raw, the fungus has a sharp, highly unpleasant, soapy flavour but cooked it is mild and good to eat. To be sure of recognising this fungus with its variable colouring preliminary tasting is essential.

The Honey Fungus is common and often abundant in late Autumn up to the first frosts. It grows in large tight clusters on stumps of old trees, on their exposed roots, or on their lower branches. It also appears in gardens on fruit trees. Gathered young, before the stem becomes woody, and growing so abundantly, it is a useful edible fungus for the late Autumn. Raw it may cause symptoms of poisoning and must therefore be thoroughly cooked, though some people are allergic to it even cooked. It is not suitable for drying. In some years really enormous quantities can be collected.

From a forestry point of view it is one of the most destructive

46

47

46. *Boletus edulis* (centre and left) p 96
47. Red capped variety, *var. fuscoruber* (right) p 96

48

48. *Boletus (Tylopilus) felleus* p 98

49

49. *Boletus badius* p 98

Edible

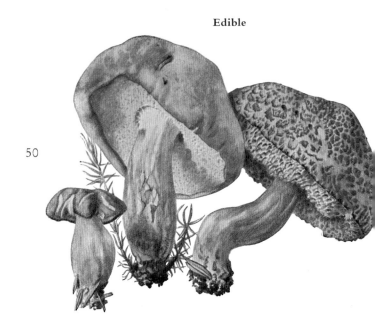

Edible

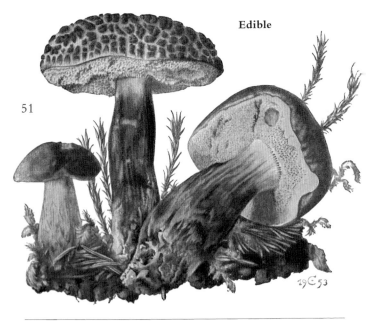

50. *Boletus subtomentosus* (upper) p 99
51. *Boletus chrysenteron* (lower) p 100

fungi, attacking wood and causing a lot of damage in woods and orchards through 'Root Rot'. When its mycelium is growing on rotten stumps or roots these emit a phosphorescent glow in the dark.

It may be confused with the *Pholiota (Kuehneromyces) mutabilis*, though without danger since this is also edible and good to eat, as well as with other edible, or at least harmless, varieties of the same species.

16. PAXILLUS INVOLUTUS

Caution

Plate 16, between pp 42 and 43 (lower)

The cap is medium sized, at first flattened-convex, then expanded to depressed, sometimes finally funnel-shaped. It is 5–12 (15) cm. wide, glistening and clammy in wet weather. It is at first downy, becoming smooth except at the margin which remains for a long time downy and is incurved with branching grooves. The colour is dull ochre-yellow to olive or reddish-brown. The gills are wide, decurrent, running well down the stem, often branched and uniting near the stem, olive-yellow to ochre-brown, very sensitive to pressure and immediately becoming dark-brown when touched. They are very easily detached from the flesh of the cap. The spore dust is ochre-yellow to red-brown, the spores yellow-brown, smooth, elliptical, 8–10μ long. The stem is solid and firm, sometimes thickened at the base, smooth, of the same colour as the cap or paler, darkening as soon as touched, 5–8 c. high, usually centrally, very occasionally eccentrically, attached. The flesh is yellow, becoming brown when touched or cut, and has a pleasant sharp taste and smell. The fungus is edible and good when young but some people are allergic to it and it is poisonous when raw. It can occasionally cause serious gastric symptoms and should therefore be thoroughly cooked.

CAP

GILLS

SPORES
STEM

It is very common from July to November growing on the ground or on stumps. It is often found in conifer woods, less often in deciduous woods, and common on heaths, pastures, in gardens and parks, and among bushes. It can hardly be confused with anything else, or at the most with a young *Paxillus atromentosus* (17) or, but only from a distance, with the *Lactarius turpis*. This is olive-green to dark olive-brown or dark green, has a sharp taste and, while it has never poisoned anybody, is edible only after suitable preparation in the cooking.

17. PAXILLUS ATROMENTOSUS

Plate 17, between pp 42 and 43 (upper)

The cap of this medium to large fungus is olive- to rust-brown, considerably inrolled, then flat to funnel-shaped, at first with a

F

velvety surface, later leathery and smooth, often cracked in dry
GILLS   weather, 8–15 (20) cm. in diameter. The gills are ochre-yellow,
compressed, decurrent, branched and then uniting, easily detached
SPORES   from the flesh of the cap. The spore dust is yellow, the spores rounded-
elliptical, pale-yellow, 5–6μ long.
STEM   The stem is short and stout, up to 6 cm. high and 4 cm. thick, with
a thick, dark-brown, velvety surface, usually eccentric to the cap.
The flesh is white to woody-yellow, soft and watery, with a sharp to
bitter taste and smell. It is edible when young. When old, tasted raw,
it has a bitter, thoroughly unpleasant inky flavour and can be
poisonous. Well cooked, with vinegar, and sliced thinly, it makes a
pleasant salad but must be avoided by those with sensitive digestions.

It grows on stumps, especially conifer stumps, from July to
October, usually singly or in small groups, and is not uncommon. It
contains a brown dye which will give a good colour to soups and
sauces. It can hardly be mistaken for any other fungus.

18. FLAMMULINA (COLLYBIA) VELUTIPES

Edible

German: WINTERPILZ   Plate 18, between pp 42 and 43

CAP   The separate caps of this fungus, which grows in clusters, are 2–10
cm. wide, thin-fleshed, smooth, sticky and glistening, honey
yellow to bright rust-yellow or orange-red, less frequently pale-
GILLS   yellow or pure white. The gills are pale-yellow, broad, the spores
SPORES   elongated, 8–10μ long. The spore dust is white. The stem is 3–8 cm.
STEM   long, fairly thin and tough, sometimes curved, hollow when old,
yellow towards the top, brown below and covered with blackish-
brown to olive-brown velvety down. It is thinner towards the base,
almost root-like and, in soft humus, sometimes with long roots. The
flesh is thin, whitish, soft, rubbery when dried and with a mild taste
and no smell.

It grows on tree-stumps and dead branches, but also on many
living trees in woods, gardens and parks, especially on old willow
stumps and currant bushes from late Autumn to March and appears
occasionally right through the year. In Winter the clusters may freeze
completely but can survive for a long time and continue to grow as
soon as mild weather comes. Like the Marasmius species, this fungus
can also dry out completely and come to life again. They are easily
cultivated.

They are edible and good, and very welcome in the Winter months
when, even frozen, they can be cooked satisfactorily and few other
fungi appear. Especially in Winter, there is no possibility of confusing
them with any dangerous species.

19. INOCYBE PATOUILLARDII

Poisonous

Plate 19, between pp 42 and 43

This small to medium-sized, often fine-looking fungus has a 2.5–8 CAP
(12) cm. wide, fleshy cap. It is at first globular, then conical to bell-
shaped, finally flattened, often wavy or bent irregularly, with radiating silky fibres and, when old, with the margin lobed or torn radially.
The colour of the cap is very variable: at first pure white and smooth,
then straw-yellow to ochre-brown. When broken or touched it turns
brick-red and when old, or kept for some time, becomes pink to GILLS
brick-red. The gills are crowded, adnexed, almost free. When young
they are whitish-pink to rust yellow, later red-brown or olive-grey,
and are finally uniformly earth-brown to brick-red. The spore dust SPPRES
is dirty-brown, the spores olive-brown, egg- to bean-shaped, 9–12 STEM
(15)µ long. The stem is 4–10 (14) cm. high, cylindrical, solid, often
curved, whitish at the top, otherwise salmon-pink to brick-red with
silky fibres and sometimes bulbous at the base. The flesh is firm and
white, yellowish soon streaked with red in the cap, finally becoming
red throughout the fungus. The smell is at first weak, later fruity. The
taste when young is nutty, when older highly unpleasant.

This dangerous fungus grows in grass especially near rivers, in
woods and clearings and also in parks and gardens from (May) June
to August (September), in small or large groups, often in the same
places, in some years sparsely, in others in large quantities.

It is deadly poisonous, and dangerous since it is found in the same
places as the *Tricholoma gambosum* (9) and the various varieties of the
Common Mushroom. It contains two-hundred times' as much
Muscarine as the Fly Agaric and, when large, can be mistaken for a
Tricholoma or even for an open *Pholiota caperata* (22). However it can
be easily identified by its earth-coloured gills and by its gradual reddening, especially after gathering. The Common Mushroom varieties
have a ring, grey-pink to chocolate-coloured gills and a pleasant
woodlike smell. The *Tricholoma gambosum* has yellow-white, non-
reddening flesh and a strongly mealy smell.

Recent research has shown that there are species of Inocybe containing little or no Muscarine. However the majority are so poisonous
and the differences so difficult to distinguish that it would be highly
dangerous to eat any of them.

20 PHOLIOTA (KUEHNEROMYCES) MUTABILIS

German: STOCKSCHWÄMMCHEN   **Edible**

Plate 20, between pp 42 and 43 (lower)

The separate caps of this fungus which grows in clusters are 3–6 (10) CAP
cm. wide, hemispherical-domed to flattened, with a blunt umbo,

smooth margins (though sometimes grooved), thin-fleshed, glistening, honey-yellow or leather-brown to cinnamon-brown. In wet
weather there is a damp, cinnamon-brown, ring-shaped zone at the
margin which remains damp for some time. The lower caps of the
cluster are usually powdered rusty-brown with spores from those
above. The gills are pale cinnamon-brown to rusty-brown, very
thick, adnate and slightly decurrent. The spores are rust-brown, egg-
shaped, smooth, 6–7μ long. The stem is 5–7 cm. high, pale, smooth,
fairly thin, tough, often curved, solid at first, later hollow, with a
membranous, flakey, transient ring, yellow-brown above, dark rust-
brown below. Below the ring the stem is dark rust-brown and scaly.
The flesh is thin, rather watery, pale-yellow in the cap, rust-brown in
the stem, with a slightly-aromatic, woody smell.

   The fungus grows from (April) May to December in many-headed
clusters on dead stumps of deciduous trees, mainly beeches, less
frequently on pines, rather scattered, though in places in large
quantities. It is edible and excellent, as flavouring in soups, sauces
and stews, to improve the flavour of other less tasty fungi, and
especially when cooked with *Craterellus cornucopioides* (29). In
spite of being so small it is very abundant since a few clusters may
contain hundreds of caps and yield a good meal. It is also easy to
cultivate.

   Other fungi with which it might be confused are either edible or
harmless but not poisonous. The *Hypholoma fasciculare* differs in having noticably green-yellow to sulpher-yellow gills and a very bitter
taste.

21. HYPHOLOMA CAPNOIDES

Edible

Plate 21, between pp 42 and 43 (upper)

CAP   This fungus also grows in clusters. The cap is 2–7 cm. wide, dull
lemon-yellow to orange-brown, smooth, hemispherical to flattened,
sometimes curved irregularly, usually rust-red in the centre, some-
GILLS   times with remnants of a whitish or dark veil at the margins. The gills
are pale white to greyish-yellow or smoky-grey, later becoming grey-
violet and blackish-brown with age. The spore dust is purple-brown
SPORES   or violet-brown, the spores the same colour, smooth, elliptical and
STEM   8–10μ long. The stem is 5–10 cm. high, thin, often curved, white to
shiny yellow, at the base darker to tawny, rust-coloured. The flesh is
firm, whitish, with a mild taste, never bitter. The smell is weak,
stronger when the fungus is dried, and reminiscent of wood, sometimes of smoked meat.

   It grows on conifer stumps throughout the year, singly in early

Spring, and in large quantities from August to November or sometimes longer. It is excellent to eat and, as it grows in clusters, very
abundant.

Beginners might confuse it only with the very bitter *Hypholoma
fasciculare* and similar species which are less good to eat but all harmless. Other similar fungi are inedible but not poisonous.

22. ROZITES (PHOLIOTA) CAPERATA

Edible

German: REIFPILZ   Plate 22, between pp 50 and 51

The cap is 5–10 (12) cm. wide and emerges from the ground with a   CAP
pale-violet, silky veil. It is globular to egg-shaped, then bell-shaped
and finally flattened. When old it is dry, curved and wrinkled, often
torn radially at the margin. It is a dingy pale-yellow, smooth, slightly
glistening, becoming straw-yellow to meal-coloured with traces of
the silvery-violet veil remaining, especially in the centre of the cap.
The dull opalescent sheen is very characteristic of this fungus. The
skin peels. The gills are crowded, clay-yellow to flesh-coloured,   GILLS
finally rust-brown and denticulate. In section the gills are white and
finely notched. The spore dust is brown, the separate spores ochre-   SPORES
yellow, almond-shaped, finely warty, 10–14μ long. The stem is 5–10   STEM
(12) cm. high, smooth, whitish, silky, almost evenly thick, solid and
firm-fleshed, flaked towards the top. Below the ring it is pale yellow,
fibrous and striated; at the base it is somewhat bulbous with a thin,   RING
pale lilac volva attached. The ring is dull-white to violet, firm and   VOLVA
enduring, at first outstanding, then hanging; narrow, membranous
and easily removable. When young a veil stretches between the margin of the cap and the stem and this later becomes the ring. The flesh

of the cap is fairly thick, whitish to yellow, sometimes pale-violet, under the centre of the cap pale-
yellow to light-orange. The flesh of the cap is
somewhat watery and membranous. The smell is
mild, the taste mild and pleasant.

This fungus appears from (July) August to the
first frosts in deciduous and sandy conifer woods,
especially under firs and pine. It is an excellent
edible fungus, unfortunately often maggoty.

In Summer care should be taken to avoid confusion with the highly-poisonous *Inocybe patouillardii* (19) which it can closely resemble when old
and opened. When young it can be mistaken for
the *Cortinarius (Inoloma) traganus* but can be distinguished by its permanent ring, colour of flesh, and
its pleasant smell.

The ring of the
*Rozites (Pholiota)
caperata*

23. RHODOPHYLLUS (ENTOLOMA) SINUATUS (LIVIDUS)

Poisonous

Plate 23, between pp 50 and 51

CAP The cap of this medium to large fungus is 6–15 (20) cm. wide, flattened-convex to expanded with a blunt umbo, sometimes undulating, dry, smooth, ivory-white to light brown or leather-coloured, grey-brown when old. It is thick-fleshed in the centre, at first with an inturned margin which is fibrous and has a silky sheen.

GILLS The gills are fairly distant, of unequal length, toothed, later free, in section undulating, at first yellow-white, then pink to salmon red.

SPORES The spore dust is flesh coloured, the spores reddish, rounded, 8–10μ

STEM long. The compact stem is 6–10 (12) cm. high, whitish, solid, powdery at the apex, thickened and with white striations at the base, hollow when old. The flesh is white, smells stongly of flour, and soon unpleasantly rancid, reminiscent of a chemist's shop. The taste is mild.

This fungus grows from May to September in deciduous woods and parks, mostly on clayey soil, under oaks and beeches, also on woodland paths and clearings and the edges of fields. It is fairly rare, but where it occurs, it grows in large quantities and often in rings. It is highly poisonous, affecting the gastric system and causing sickness and long-lasting after effects. It is found beside many edible fungi: the St. George's Mushroom (9), the gills of which are, however, crowded and remain whitish-yellow; the *Clitopilus prunulus,* the gills of which are decurrent and the spores usually large with six longtitudinal grooves; in late Autumn with the *Aspropaxillus giganteus,* the gills of which are also decurrent; the *Clitocybe geotropa,* the *Clitocybe nebularis* (14) and with the *Pluteus cervinus.* Beginners should be careful. See chapter 'Fungus Poisoning', p. 37.

24. THE HORSE MUSHROOM

Agaricus arvensis

French: BOULE DE NEIGE   **Edible**
German: SCHAF–EGERLING   Plate 24, between pp 50 and 51

CAP The cap is 5–15 (20) cm. wide, at first closed, then egg- to bell-shaped becoming hemispherical and finally domed to flattened, white to creamy-white, at first tufted or finely flaked, then smooth with a silky sheen–often tattered when dry–and often with remnants of the veil at the margin. The skin becomes yellowish when bruised and

GILLS does not always peel easily. The gills are small, crowded, unequal in length, narrowing slightly at the stem, at first pale grey to flesh-coloured or grey pink, then red-brown becoming dark chocolate-

SPORES brown with age. The spore-dust is dark chocolate-brown, the spores

purple-brown, egg-shaped, 5–8μ long. The slender, evenly-thick STEM
stem is 5–16 cm. high, white, showing yellow spots where bruised,
bulbous at the base, at first solid, later slightly hollow, with a thick,
tough, two-layered downward-hanging ring with radiating star-
shaped patches below, white inside, tufted or rough outside. The flesh
is firm though tender, remaining white, and only the flesh of the stem
turns a tawny-brown with age. There is a pleasant aniseed or almond
smell, the taste is mild, nutty.

The Horse Mushroom grows from July to October on low-lying
ground, often at the edges of conifer woods, in clearings, under bushes
in parks, and also on pastures and meadows used by cattle, but seldom
in thick woods. It is an excellent, edible fungus. A more slender,
related species is the *Agaricus silvicolus* with a simple ring and the
flesh of the stem brown to blackish when old. The bulb at the base is
markedly flattened. It is not common.

These should not be confused with the *Agaricus xanthodermus*–The
Yellow-Staining Mushroom–or with the *Agaricus meleagris* which
have an inky, carbolic or iodine smell and are slightly poisonous.

Confusion with the Death Cap (1) or with the *Amanita virosa* (2)
could be fatal. Both of these have permanently white gills, prominent
rings and bulbous bases with volvas.

In early Summer the *Inocybe patouillardii* (19), which is at first pure
white but slowly becomes brick-red, with earth-coloured gills and
an unpleasant smell, is also a very dangerous possible double.

25. THE FIELD MUSHROOM

Agaricus campestris

French: ROSÉ DES PRÉS
Italian: PRATAIOLO,
Spanish: SETA DE CAMPO, **Edible**
German: WIESEN-EGERLING Plate 25, facing p 51 (upper)

The cap is normally medium-sized, thick, 3–10 cm. wide, at first CAP
closed and nearly spherical, then domed for some time and finally
flattened, typically white to dull-white or brownish, sometimes
slightly yellow, silky-filamentous to flaky, inturned, often overhang-
ing at the margin, with remains of the veil hanging down. The gills GILLS
are wide, free, crowded, pinkish to salmon-coloured, finally dark-
chocolate or almost black, and moist. The spore-dust is black-brown,
the spores dark purple-brown, elongated, 7–8 (10)μ long. The fairly SPORES
short stem, only 3–7 cm. long is at first solid, then stuffed, of even STEM
thickness slightly tapering at the base, sometimes yellowing, generally
white to light pink and later darker, with a transient ring which is RING
white, thin, often fringed at the edge and rather scaly underneath. The
base of the stem is sometimes encircled by traces of the veil. The flesh

is white and tender and only when old, especially in the stem, toned
reddish or orange-yellow. There is a slight, pleasant smell reminiscent
of fresh-sawn wood, sometimes also of plums. The taste is mild, nutty.
This is the well-known wild, edible mushroom and excellent to eat.

It occurs in good years as early as (May) June to October, often in
quantities, on meadows and pastures, also in gardens, less frequently
in woods. In dry years it appears on heaps of horse-manure, after
heavy rain often in large quantities. Since there are several varieties it
is often confused with other Agarics, sometimes with the more rare
Lepiota naucina which is also edible and good, smells strongly of fruit,
is very slender, and has a moveable, very transient ring. The Agarics
can easily be recognised by the grey-pink to chocolate-brown gills
but very young fungi may cause difficulty. Great care is needed on
pasture land near woods to avoid possible confusion with the Death
Cap since this mistake can be deadly. It should be emphasised once
again that most fungus poisoning occurs through this confusion.

26. AGARICUS SILVATICUS
(Brown Wood Mushroom)

French: PSALLIOTE DES FORÊTS   **Edible**
German: WALD-EGERLING   Plate 26, facing p 51 (lower)

CAP   The cap is 4–10 (12) cm. wide, light cinnamon-brown, bell-shaped to
hemispherical, then domed and finally flattened, with ochre to dark-
brown fibrous scales on a white surface, often flecked with red and
red-brown, thick fleshed, but thin and often torn at the margin. The
GILLS   gills are thick, narrowing at each end, pale lilac-grey to grey-red,
reddening immediately when touched or cut, finally chocolate-brown
SPORES   and white-tufted in section. The spore dust is dark brown with spores
of the same colour, $4.5–8\mu$ long and elliptical. The white, occasionally
STEM   brown-flaked stem which reddens when touched is cylindrical, bulb-
RING   ous at the base, at first solid, then hollow with a thin ring, first white
to pink, white underneath, smoky-brown when old, lying low down
on the stem. The whitish flesh quickly turns red and later brown. The
smell is mild, rather woody and the taste mild, though sometimes
rather musty and earthy.

The *Agaricus silvaticus* grows from July to October in conifer
woods, sometimes in large numbers, and is often overlooked since it
tones with the ground. It is a good edible fungus, especially in combination with others.

It can be confused with other edible Agarics, especially with the
more rare *Agaricus haemorrhoidarius*–though this has salmon-red gills
and flesh which becomes at once bright salmon-red when cut.

It may also be confused with dark-toned specimens of the *Agaricus
bisporus* with grey-brown to dull dark-brown, scaly, radially-fibrous
cap which is 10 cm. wide, spherical, then bell-shaped to flattened,

52

52. *Boletus luteus* p 101

53. *Boletus granulatus* p 101

54

54. *Boletus satanus* p 102

55

55. *Boletus erythropus* (centre and below) p 103
56. *Boletus luridus* (upper) p 104

torn at the margin and with remnants of the veil attached. Its gills are crowded, flesh-pink to chocolate-brown, tufted white in section. The white, smooth stem is stuffed to hollow with a thick skinny, upstanding, rough-edged ring near the base of the stem which can be moved downwards. The white flesh becomes red when touched or torn, smells of fresh wood or plums, and has a mild taste. The 4–7μ rounded and smooth spores are in pairs on the basidia. It grows mainly outside woods on manure heaps and compost, in gardens and at the roadside from July to October, sometimes in quantity and is a good edible mushroom though with much less flavour than the wild field mushroom.

27. THE SHAGGY CAP OR LAWYER'S WIG

Coprinus comatus

French: GOUTTE D'ENCRE,
Spanish: COPRINOS CABELLUDOS,   **Edible**
German: SCHOPF–TINTLING   Plate 27, facing p 58

The cap is 5–8 (15) cm. high and 3–4 cm. wide, egg- to candle-shaped   CAP
and finally open, at first lying close to the stem, pure white though soon pinkish to blackish at the margin, with raised white and brownish fibrous scales, often sticky and with brown firm skin at the tip. The thin crowded gills are narrow at each end, free, at first pure white   GILLS
but soon pink at the margin, becoming purple-pink to brown and finally inky black. They soon deliquesce from the bottom to an ink-like fluid. In section they are whitish. The spores dust is black, the   SPORES
spores smooth, egg-shaped 12–16μ long. The 10–20 cm. high stem is   STEM
white, with fine fibres, hollow but firm, and there is a narrow, movable, often very transient, white ring which at first, in young fungi, encloses the margin of the cap. (See Diagram). The flesh is soft, white and very delicate but soon colours. Smell and taste are slight, mild and pleasant.

This fungus, looking as though modelled in porcelain, is common from April to November by the roadside and in ditches, on rubbish and compost heaps, in well-manured meadows, in gardens and along woodland paths, especially cattle tracks. When young, while the gills are still white or pale pink, it is an excellent edible fungus. As well as being good in soups and stews it is excellent for mushroom ketchup. It can be confused – though without any danger – with its grey relatives, especially the *Corprinus atramentarius*. It is unwise to drink alcohol when eating Shaggy Caps.

The closed-cap stage of the Shaggy Cap (*Coprinus comatus*) showing future, transient ring

28. THE FAIRY RING CHAMPIGNON

Marasmius oreades

French: MOUSSERON D'AUTOMNE,   **Edible**
German: FELD-SCHWINDLING Plate 28, between pp 58 and 59 (upper)

CAP

GILLS
SPORES
STEM

This small fungus has a 3–6 cm. wide, cone-shaped to domed, then flattened, cap with a stumpy umbo. The skin is smooth on top, pale yellow or tan when dry, ochre to buff-coloured when wet, sometimes slightly tattered at the margins. The gills are whitish, almost free, crowded, wide, distant and unequal in length. The spores are white, egg-shaped to pip-shaped, 7–9µ long. The thin stem is 4–8 cm. high, whitish, solid, rigid and tough, felty to flaky, or smooth. The flesh is pale ochre, with a pleasant aromatic smell like freshly-sawn wood and the taste is mild and nutty.

The Fairy Ring Champignon appears from July to November on commons, paths and the edges of woods, as well as on lawns, meadows and heaths, often in large numbers, growing in Fairy Rings. It is edible and tasty, especially good for soups and stews, its small size being compensated for by the fact that large quantities can be gathered. The tough stems should be discarded. It is very suitable for drying and powdering as flavouring. It can dry out completely and come to life again after rain, but only fresh caps and not those which had previously dried, should be gathered. It is easy to cultivate and after a certain time gives good results. It is sometimes confused with the *Collybia peronata* (= *Marasmius urens*) which is harmless but of little use, and also with the *Collybia dryophila,* which is so varied in shape and colour that even experts are confused. This is also harmless, though not always digestible.

29. THE HORN OF PLENTY

Craterellus cornucopioides

French: CORNE D'ABONDANCE,
Italian: CORNO DELL'ABONDANZIA,
Spanish: CUERNO DE LA ABUDANCIA,   **Edible**
German: HERBST-TROMPETE.   Plate 29, between pp 58 and 59 (lower)

SHAPE

The fruit-body is up to 15 cm. high and 3–7 cm. wide, trumpet- or funnel-shaped, rather like a drinking horn, the margin turned down, often undulating and crinkled. There is no separate stem and the fungus is hollow to its base. The outside, with the fruit-layer, is smooth, then slightly wrinkled, then with branching folds. The colour is dull ash-grey to blue-violet, darker, almost black, in wet weather and finally, due to the spores, with white grooves. The spores are elliptical, 10–13μ long, smooth and whitish. The flesh is thin, tough when old and almost woody, with a slight smell and, when raw, a not-unpleasant earthy taste.

The Horn Of Plenty occurs from (July) August to late Autumn (November) in beech and oak woods—less frequently in conifer woods—on damp ground and keeping to the same habitats.

It is good cooked with other fungi and especially good for flavouring, and so is best used in powder forms in soups and stews. Otherwise it should be cut into small pieces for cooking.

Very similar to The Horn Of Plenty is the *Cantharellus cinereus*. This has a narrow, tubular stem with well separated, blue-grey, branching grooves on the outer surface and grows in clusters in deciduous woods. It is rather rare, though frequent in places, and is also edible.

30. THE SAFFRON MILK CAP

Lactarius deliciosus

German : EDELREIZRER **Edible**
Italian : LAPACENDRO BUONO Plate 30, between pp 58 and 59 (lower)

The cap of this stout and thick-fleshed fungus is flat dome-shaped, at CAP first with incurved margin, then flattened with a depression in the centre becoming funnel-shaped and sometimes undulating. The surface is smooth, never matted, the colour bright-orange to carrot-red with darker circular rings, showing verdigris spots where touched or cut and, finally, pale-green when old. The skin is bare, often slightly clammy, and will not peel. The gills are decurrent, thick, wide, stiff GILLS and fragile, unequal in length, branching, orange-yellow to saffron and specked with green where bruised. The spore dust is light-ochre, the spores elliptical, warty, 8–10μ long. The stem is 2–7 cm. high, SPORES evenly thick, smooth, soon hollow, very stiff and brittle, yellow- to STEM brick-red, often tinged with green by the milky juice. The flesh is firm but very brittle, whitish, but soon discoloured by the plentiful, mild-tasting, saffron to orange milk and becomes specked with green. The smell is pleasantly aromatic, the taste usually mild and savoury.

This fungus occurs on clayey soil, on heaths and woodland clearings and in conifer woods, in groups and often in large quantities, from July to October. It is best fried or grilled, or used as flavouring and is less satisfactory for soups or prepared as a vegetable. It cannot be used dry, but is good for salads, preserved in salt, or for making mushroom extract. Unfortunately it is often maggoty. Sometime it has a strong resiny flavour and is then useless for cooking. Many people prefer it to the related *Lactarius sanguifluus*. This has wine-red to flesh-coloured gills, blue-green zones, and wine-red to blood-red milk. Its stem is solid. When torn it turns blood-red, specked with verdigris. This is an excellent edible fungus but much rarer than the *Lactarius deliciosus*.

Both the above may be confused with the *Lactarius torminosus* (31) which is poisonous when raw.

31. THE WOOLLY MILK CAP

Lactarius torminosus

Caution

German: BIRKENREIZKER   Plate 31, between pp 58 and 59 (upper)

CAP The cap is rather thin-fleshed, 3–8 (15) cm. wide, flattened concave, at first and for some time with an inrolled margin, then expanded to downpressed and finally often funnel-shaped. The edge of the cap is covered with shaggy woolly fibrils. The cap is slimy when moist, pale pink to flesh-coloured or brownish, with regular circular darker GILLS zones. The gills are crowded, decurrent and remain pinkish-yellow. SPORES The spores are whitish and warty to rough, 8–10μ long. The evenly-STEM thick stem is 3–8 cm. high, porous but solid, later hollow, light flesh-coloured, in places pitted. The flesh of the cap is rosy to brown, very brittle, with a considerable quantity of permanently white, acrid milk. The smell is weak, slightly reminiscent of turpentine, the taste is acrid, resinous and bitter.

The Woolly Milk Cap appears from August to October in woods, especially under beeches, on woodland paths and heaths. Raw it is an irritant if not definitely poisonous but it is edible after suitable pre-paration and is eaten in Northern Europe. However as it needs special treatment it cannot be recommended for general consumption.

Sometimes a fungus will be found which appears to be either a Lactarius or a Russula, but which has no gills. These specimens are then differently, often more vividly coloured. In these cases the gills have been prevented from forming by a microscopic parasite fungus and such specimens should be avoided.

32. LACTARIUS VOLEMUS

French: VACHETTE   **Edible**
German: MILCHBRÄTLING   Plate 32, facing p 59

CAP The cap of this fine looking fungus is 5–15 (20) cm. wide, at first globular, then flattened-convex, when young with an inturned margin, soon becoming depressed to funnel-shaped in the centre, dull velvety to smooth and dry, golden yellow to bright orange, and without darker zones. The skin does not peel. The thick, pale-yellow, rather crowded, firm and brittle gills are slightly decurrent and when GILLS damaged release white, sticky milk, turning grey in the air, which stains the gills and fingers brown. The spore dust is white, the spores SPORES white, round, rough, 8–9µ long. The stem is evenly thick, white to STEM yellow, firm and full, slightly grooved, rounded at the base. The flesh is thick, white to yellow, firm and rather tough. There is at first a sweetish smell of honey or pear blossom, later the smell is lobster-like and, when old, like fish oil or herrings. The taste is mild and pleasant and the fungus can be eaten raw provided there is no fishy smell.

It grows from July to October in deciduous and conifer woods, mostly singly but, in moist places, in quantity. It is a good edible fungus, well suited to quick frying or grilling. It is best slightly salted, stuffed, rolled in flour and baked. Stewed it is disappointing, sometimes becoming slimy and unappetising. It is not suitable for drying, but good in salads and preserved in vinegar or salt for winter use. Its smell alone prevents confusion with other Lactarius species which are mostly smaller and have an acrid taste.

33. LACTARIUS PIPERATUS

French: LACTAIRE POIVRÉ **Edible**
German: PFEFFER-MILCHLING Plate 33, facing p 66

This fungus is often very thick and firm-fleshed. The cap is usually CAP fairly regular, 5–10 (20) cm. wide, dry, smooth, flattened-convex to flattened when young, at first with markedly-inturned margin, then concave to funnel-shaped, sometimes scarred, without zones. The colour is white or ivory, sometimes specked with brown. The gills GILLS are very crowded, rather thick, very narrow, branching, whitish to yellowish and decurrent. The spore dust is white, the spores white, SPORES almost spherical, rough, 6–8.5µ long. The stem is slender and firm, STEM 3–6 (10) cm. high, smooth or slightly grooved, solid and stiff, often eccentric to the cap, narrowing at the base. The flesh is white, firm, fragile and has an abundance of white, strongly peppery milk. The smell is mildly aromatic.

The *Lactarius piperatus* is common in deciduous woods, especially under beeches from July to October. It is harmless and reputed to be inedible, but has a tart, not unpleasant, unusual flavour when fried with butter, bacon and onions. It can also be salted down and the flesh then turns greenish-grey. It is quite unsuited to stews. It is reputed to affect the bladder and has been prescribed for gall-stones (p. 57).

It can only be confused with the very similar, often still larger, irregularly-curved *Lactarius vellereus* which differs in having markedly distant gills, a fibrous woolly skin and a short thick stem. The milk is bitingly acrid. Although some people do appreciate the *Lactarius piperatus* in spite of its pungency, this is not the case with the *Lactarius velleus*. However it is better than its reputation and perfectly edible.

34. RUSSULA CYANOXANTHA

Edible

French: CHARBONNIER   Plate 34, between pp 66 and 67 (lower)

CAP   The cap of this impressive fungus is 5–12 (15) cm. wide, at first hemispherical, then flattened, sometimes scarred, finally concave, often a little wavy. It is smooth, sometimes radially veined, sticky when wet, glistening and dry when old. The colour is very variable varying from pale lilac to violet, or green-violet to dark green, becoming paler with age. The skin is often slightly grooved at the margin and peels one-third of the way inwards from the margin. The

GILLS   gills are white, almost crowded, wide, narrowing at each end, very soft and elastic, branched, adnate and pointed at the inner end. Sections of the gills and stem often show milky drops when young.

SPORES   The spore dust is pure white, the spores elliptical, warty, 7–10µ long.

STEM   The stem is white, more rarely tinged with lilac, 5–10 cm. high, smooth, solid and thick-fleshed to stuffed, cylindrical, slightly veined, usually narrowing at the base. The flesh is thick, pure white, brownish when old, violet under the skin of the cap, and granular. There is no smell. The taste is pleasant and nutty.

This fungus is common in deciduous and conifer woods on chalky ground, especially under beeches, from June to November, growing usually singly but in some places abundantly. It is very well-flavoured, excellent to eat and is popular in markets on the Continent.

Very similar is the smaller *Russula grisea,* with pale-yellow gills, reddish stem and reddish flesh under the centre of the cap. Its gills are brittle, reddish in section. This is also a good edible fungus but is seldom recognised and nearly always confused with the *Russula cyanoxantha*.

35. RUSSULA VESCA

Edible

German: SPEISE-TÄUBLING   Plate 35, between pp 66 and 67 (upper)

CAP   The cap is 5–10 cm. wide, hemispherical to flat, fairly regular, depressed in the centre, slightly scarred, and when young with a sharp margin which is seldom curved. When it first appears it is usually very pale, almost white, but when mature becomes flesh-coloured, pink to red, lilac-violet, and red-brown to blood red. When old it often grows paler. It is finely grooved with radial veins, almost always with rust-coloured spots and, when old, 1–2 cm. of the margin is free from skin. The skin of the cap is mat, dry and heavy and usually peels only midway from the margin. The gills are whitish, crowded, narrow and thin, stiff and very brittle, unequal in length, forked, adnate and slightly decurrent. When old the gills are brown-flecked with drops of liquid and also have large grey spots. The spore dust is white, the spores fairly small, 6–8μ long, rounded, pear-shaped, with fine warts. The stem is 4–7 cm. high, cylindrical, sometimes rounded in the centre and wrinkled. It is at first firm, then spongy, white, sometimes tinged with pink, narrowing near the base and nearly always specked with brown. It dyes a bright red with ferrous sulphate. There is almost no smell, the taste is mild and pleasant, rather like hazel nuts.

GILLS

SPORES
STEM

The *Russula vespa* grows from June to October in conifer and deciduous woods, especially under oaks and beeches, singly and not very abundantly, usually at the edges of woods and on woodland paths. It is one of the best-flavoured edible fungi and is also edible raw. The reddish colour of the cap–similar to smoked meat–the margin bare of skin, as well as the brown spots on skin and gills distinguish this fungus from other edible Russulas. It is resembled by the green, edible *Russula heterophylla,* but this is olive-green to olive-brown and the spores are only 5–6μ long. Beginners should be very careful not to confuse this with the Death Cap (1).

36. RUSSULA FELLEA

Caution

Plate 36, between pp 66 and 67 (upper)

This fungus is small and very brittle. The cap is 3–7 cm. wide, hemispherical to flat when opened, thin-fleshed, striated at the margin when old, mostly dry and mat. The colour is pale ochre-yellow to straw-yellow, in the centre of the cap dull ochre-brown to orange-red. The skin peels only at the margins. The gills are similarly coloured, thick, small and thin, adnate, and exude drops of moisture. The spore dust is whitish-yellow, the spores white, elliptical, coarsely-warted, 8–9μ long. The stem is short, 2–6 cm. in length, nearly the same colour as the cap, smooth, firm, solid to stuffed, finally hollow. The flesh is pale yellow, brittle and fragile, the smell sweetish reminiscent of mustard oil, the taste bitter, unbearably hot and acrid.

CAP

GILLS

SPORES
STEM

The *Russula fellea* occurs from July to October in deciduous woods, more rarely among conifers, but frequently and sometimes abundantly under beeches and oaks. Beginners often confuse it with the *Russula ochroleuca* (37) from which it is distinguished by its small size, firmness and fragility; its general pale-yellow tone, the noticeable smell and the extremely acrid taste. The *Russula fellea* is completely inedible and slightly poisonous. Somewhat resembling it is the rare *Russula solaris*. The cap of this is bright-yellow with red tones, and rather bulbous. Its spore dust is cream, the spores 7–8μ, with pointed warts. It also smells of mustard oil.

37. RUSSULA OCHROLEUCA

Plate 37, between pp 66 and 67 (lower)

CAP   The cap is 4–8 (10) cm. wide, hemispherical to flattened, but often depressed and sometimes concave and wavy, smooth, sticky, lemon- to honey-yellow, often olive-brown to green in the centre, becoming paler with age. The margin is at first smooth and, when old, slightly GILLS   striated. The skin of the cap peels half-way from the margin. The gills are white to yellow, almost free, fairly distant, almost equally long, SPORES   sometimes tinged with brown. The spore dust is white, the spores elliptical, spiny, 8–10μ long. In section the gills and skin show large STEM   quantities of cystidia. The stem is whitish-yellow, 3–8 cm. high, cylindrical, when old greyish, the surface wrinkled and net-like. The flesh is white and firm, when old, grey and spongy, brittle and yellow under the skin of the cap. The smell is mildly fruity and pleasant, the taste only moderately acrid, sometimes almost mild.

The *Russula ochroleuca* grows from July to October in deciduous and conifer woods, especially under firs, and is very common and often found in large quantities. It is by far the most common of the Russulas. From the point of view of edibility it is of little value though it can be eaten, mixed with other fungi or (first well-simmered in water) in salads. The sharpness which it has when raw is almost completely lost in cooking.

It is often confused with the similar, but inedible, *Russula fellea* (36), which is however mainly found in beechwoods. Very similar is the *Russula claroflava* which only grows under birch and alders. It has a much brighter yellow cap, a mainly yellow stem, and a fruity smell. The spores are 7–9μ long and warty, and cap and stem become grey. It is a good edible fungus.

38. RUSSULA INTEGRA

Edible

Plate 38, between pp 66 and 67 (upper)

CAP   The cap is 6–12 cm. wide, hemispherical to domed, finally depressed and undulating, clammy and for some time glistening, smooth, yellow-brown to olive-brown or chocolate- to purple-brown, often

Caution

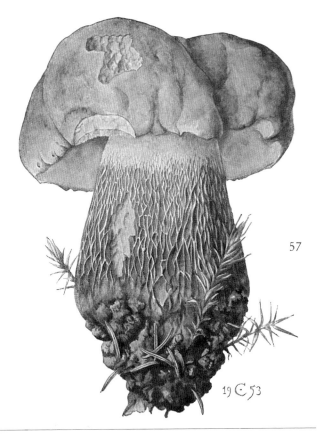

57

57. *Boletus calopus* p 104

Edible

58

59

Edible

58. *Boletus scaber* (left) p 105
59. *Boletus versipellis* (right) p 105

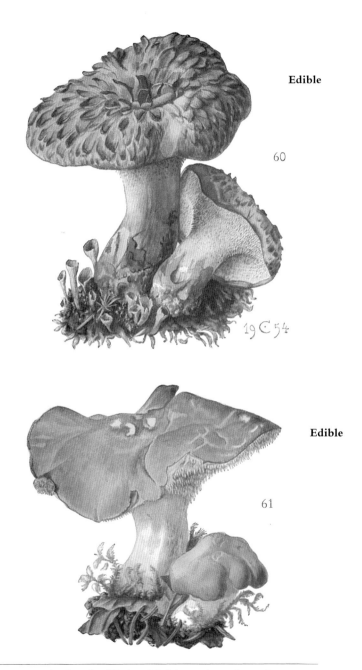

Edible

60

19 C 54

Edible

61

60. *Sarcodon (Hydnum) imbricatum* (upper) p 106
61. *Hydnum (Sarcodon) repandum* (lower) p 107

**Edible
when young**

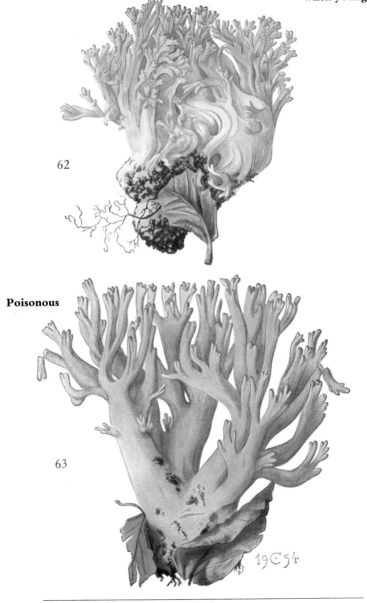

62

Poisonous

63

19C54

62 *Clavaria (Ramaria) aurea* (upper) p 107
63. *Clavaria (Ramaria) pallida* (lower) p 108

paler yellow in the centre of the cap and usually with pronounced striation at the margin. The skin peels up to two-thirds from the margin. The gills are wide and thick, pale-white for some time and, when old, yellow to ochre-yellow. In section and also on the skin are numerous cystidia which dye blue in sulphovanillin. The spore dust is ochre-yellow, the single spores pale-ochre, 10–12µ long, elliptical and spiny. The stem is firm and stout, sometimes swollen, usually pure white, less frequently reddish, 3–9 cm. in length, smooth, silky, veined, often tinged with yellow at the base. The flesh is white, mild, only occasionally slightly acrid, without smell or smelling slightly of fruit, usually tasting somewhat of almonds. It dyes brown in carbolic acid.

GILLS

SPORES
STEM

This fungus is common from June to November in deciduous woods. It is edible, excellent and well-flavoured, though somewhat tough. The sticky skin is almost always covered with leaves and earth but is fairly easily cleaned.

The *Russula integra* is often confused, without any danger, with the excellent, edible *Russula mustelina,* and unfortunately also with the deceptively similar, unpleasant *Russula badia*. When the gills of this are rubbed they smell like cigar box wood. The taste is at first mild but then extremely acrid, almost unbearable, and long lasting. It is found only on mouldy soil under conifers and its taste should be sufficient identification.

39. RUSSULA VIRESCENS

Edible

French: PALOMET   Plate 39, between pp 66 and 67 (lower)

The cap is 5–15 cm. wide, at first closed and spherical to hemi-spherical, then domed to flattened, sometimes depressed in the centre, warty or scarred, with a smooth, blunt, and sometimes ribbed, margin. The skin is dry, at first white, then pale green to yellow or verdigris-coloured, or even grey-green, and finally pales to yellow-green. It has a granular surface which becomes cracked and broken into patches. When moist, half to three-quarters of the skin can be peeled from the margin. The gills are pale white, free, fairly crowded, very brittle, unequal in length and branched. The spore dust is white, the spores white, rounded, only 5–7µ long, slightly rough or spiny. The stem is white, usually of even thickness, 3–10 cm. high and always slightly grooved. The flesh is white, firm to brittle, the taste mild, nutty and pleasant. The smell is often barely noticeable or slightly fruity, when old reminiscent of herrings.

CAP

GILLS

SPORES
STEM

The fungus occurs from July to October in conifer and mixed woods and under bushes, and singly or in numbers under birches, oaks and beeches. It is a good edible fungus, especially fried or grilled, and prized by some people as the best of the Russulas and as good as *Boletus edulis*. When young it is not always recognised since it is quite white when it appears above ground, and it can then only be identified by its firmness and nutty taste. Later its colour and the cracked surface make confusion with other fungi unlikely.

40. THE SICKENER
Russula emetica

Caution

Plate 40, between pp 66 and 67

CAP The fungus is generally small but can grow to an impressive size. The cap is 3–8 (10) cm. wide, thin-fleshed, brittle, at first hemispherical then convex to flattened, sometimes depressed, often with coarse striations at the margin. The skin is sticky, glistening in wet weather, rather wrinkled when dry, and peels almost completely when moist. The colour is very varied: bright red, cherry-red, blood-red and purple-red, often black in the centre, and finally often pale. The gills are pure white, sometimes grey white, equal in length, adnate to free, distant and fairly elastic, seldom breaking. The spore dust is white or yellow-white, the spores white, rounded, 8–10μ long, with a netlike arrangement of spines. In section, but also on the skin of cap and stem, are numerous cystidia tapering at each end. The stem is mostly rather short, 5–8 cm high, smooth, pure white, firm, solid and elastic when young; when old spongy-soft and very brittle. The flesh is thin, pure white, reddish under the skin of the cap, at first firm but soon fragile, becoming elastic on keeping. It smells pleasantly of dried fruit and first tastes somewhat mild, but very soon extremely acrid and burning, with a bitter after-taste. Cooked it is mild.

GILLS

SPORES

STEM

Since the *Russula emetica* is extremely varied it is not always easily distinguished from other red species. It occurs from June (July) to November in deciduous and conifer woods or on heaths and moors, usually on moss in damp places. It is poisonous raw, causing sickness and diarrhoea, but the poison can be destroyed by cooking and it is eaten in Northern Europe after careful washing and well simmering. However, there are so many good edible and harmless fungi that it is wise to avoid this one. The *Russula fragilis*, which is also slightly poisonous, is very similar to it. The gills of this are notched in section and its stem dyes blue on the surface with naphthol. Many red Russulas are very similar to these two and a taste test is therefore essential. In general there is the rule: 'All mild tasting Russulas are edible', but anyone who cannot yet distinguish a Russula ought not to collect any gill-fungi since confusion might cause death.

41. HYGROPHORUS (CAMAROPHYLLUS) PRATENSIS

Edible

German: WIESEN-ELLERLING   Plate 41, between pp 66 and 67

This fungus is small to medium-sized, in shape like a child's top. The cap is 3–7 (10) cm. wide, at first bell-shaped, then domed and CAP flattened, finally depressed to concave in the centre, smooth and dry, light-yellow to ochre-yellow, also leather-yellow to tawny-orange, with a sharp thin margin which is moist in wet weather. When moist it can from above resemble a *Pholiota mutabilis* (20). The gills are GILLS very distant, thick, waxy, branching, very decurrent and usually the same colour as the cap. The spores are elliptical, colourless, 6–7μ long. SPORES The spore dust is white. The stem is 4-8 cm. high, gradually thicken- STEM ing and merging into the cap, narrowing towards the base, smooth and pale ochre-yellow. The flesh is pale yellow to orange-yellow, watery and almost without smell. The taste is mild and pleasant.

This fungus occurs only in Autumn, from September to October (November) on the edges of woods and in woodland meadows, also on pastures and grassy clearings or slopes, as well as on heaths, but nearly always near woods, in places abundantly and keeping to the same habitats. It is an extremely good edible fungus but is not very well known, since in the Autumn, fungi hunters look mainly in woods. Those who know its habitats and have eaten it like it best cooked by itself. Because of its shape, colour, and habitat it can hardly be confused with any other fungus.

Somewhat similar in shape, but white is the *Hygrophorus virgineus.* It is also only small to medium-sized, but thick-fleshed, with a pleasant taste. Somewhat larger is the *Hygrophorus camarophyllus* with black fibrous striations on a rust-grey cap, white gills becoming grey to green with age, rust-coloured fibrous stem and white, mild flesh. This is a first-class edible fungus and grows in conifer woods.

42. GOMPHIDIUS GLUTINOSUS

Edible

German: ROTZER   Plate 42, between pp 66 and 67 (right)

The cap of this fungus, shaped very like a child's top, is 5–10 cm. CAP wide, smooth, hemispherical, domed to flattened, finally cone-shaped, often with inrolled margin, grey-brown to violet or almost chocolate, paler when old and then often spotted black. When young the fungus is covered over the whole surface of the cap, the margin, the gills and the under-surface of the cap with a transparent, clammy veil which soon tears at the margin of the cap and extends in strands, VEIL rather like a cobweb, to the top of the stem. After tearing completely

GILLS

SPORES

it remains there for a time as a clammy ring, blackened by the spores. The gills are thick, wide and soft, rather waxy, fairly distant, branched, deeply decurrent, and are at first whitish, soon grey, and finally blackened by the spores. The surface of the gills appears to be hairy (cystidia). The gills are easily detached from the flesh of the cap. The spore dust is black, the single spores spindly, very large, 18–20μ long and black-brown. The flesh is soft, whitish to dirty-grey, brittle in the stem, bright lemon-yellow at the base of the stem, without noticeable smell and with a mild taste.

This fungus grows fairly abundantly in conifer woods from July to October and can be found at the edges of the woods, in clearings, and especially under young firs. It is a good edible fungus, not suited to drying, but excellent in soups and stews. In woods it may easily be mistaken for the *Boletus luteus* (52) or for the *Boletus granulatus* until examination and removal of the clammy veil reveals gills instead of tubes. It is seldom attacked by maggots. It should be cleaned when first picked and the clammy veil removed, since it is usually covered with pine-needles, leaves and specks of dirt, and dirties the other fungi which have been gathered. With practice, the skin of the cap can be removed in one movement.

Similar to the *Gomphidius glutinosus* is the 3–8 cm. wide, also edible, much rarer, *Gomphidius maculatus* with pink to pale-red cap. Its smoky black gills colour wine-red or brown when touched and its slimy veil soon disappears. Its stem is flecked with reddish-brown spots by the yellow to blood-red drops which it exudes and its flesh and stem colour wine-red when broken. Its spores are 17–21 (23)μ long.

43. GOMPHIDIUS RUTILUS (VISCIDUS)

Edible

Plate 43, between pp 66 and 67 (left)

CAP

GILLS

SPORES

STEM

This fungus is medium-sized and the shape of a child's top. The cap is 4–12 cm wide, at first cone- to bell-shaped, then flattened, with a pointed umbo, not clammy, smooth to finely-flaked, copper-red or wine-red becoming pale with age. The gills are thick, wedge-shaped in section, distant, deeply decurrent, orange-red to grey-red or chocolate when young, often flesh-coloured in section. The spore dust is brown, the spores 18–24μ long. The stem is 5–10 cm. high, somewhat lighter than the cap, at first almost ringed with fibrous scales, narrowing, and saffron-yellow towards the base. The flesh is orange-yellow to reddish and yellower at the base. It is an excellent edible fungus.

It is found from July to October (November) in conifer woods, especially under pines, keeping to the same habitats but only in places abundant.

44. THE CHANTERELLE
Cantharellus cibarius

French: CHANTERELLE BLONDE, GIROLE.
Italian: GALLINACCIO.   **Edible**
German: PFIFFERLING.   Plate 44, facing p 67 (upper)

This small though sometimes quite impressive fungus is more-or-less
funnel-shaped. The cap is 2–8 cm. wide, first domed with inturned   CAP
edge, then flattened becoming depressed in the centre, then funnel-
shaped or top-shaped, often irregularly lobed and undulating. The
skin does not peel. Dwarf or giant varieties which do sometimes occur
are variants due to local conditions. The stem is pale yellow to egg-   STEM
yellow, sometimes becoming paler, tapering towards the base,
2–6 cm. high, stout and fleshy. The fold-like gills are distant, narrow,   GILLS
thickish, blunt-edged, branched and re-uniting and are deeply decurrent, running a considerable way down the stem. The spore dust is
pale ochre-yellow, the spores elliptical, 7–11µ long. The entire fungus   SPORES
is more-or-less egg-yellow though sometimes paler. The flesh is pale
yellow with yellow edges, has an aromatic, apricot-like smell, and
a mild taste with a slight peppery aftertaste.

On the Continent this is one of the best-known edible fungi,
frequently sold in shops, and it deserves to be equally appreciated
here. It occurs, often in large numbers, in deciduous and conifer
woods, especially near firs, from June to October. It lasts well, is
seldom attacked by maggots and is particularly good to eat, though
dried it is only suitable to be powdered as a flavouring.

Very similar to the Chanterelle is the *Hygrophoropsis aurantica*. The
gills of this are branched but do not re-unite and the stem is sometimes
at one side. This is more orange than egg-yellow, its cap is velvety and
the flesh much thinner. It is edible but not very tasty. It does not have
the apricot scent of the Chanterelle.

45. GOMPHUS CLAVATUS
(Cantharellus clavatus Person)

Edible
Plate 45, facing p 67 (lower)

This fungus is roughly irregularly club- or funnel-shaped or sometimes partly ear-shaped, thick-fleshed, with a short stem, up to 10 cm.
high and 6 cm. across. The cap is violet-purple soon becoming   CAP
greeny-yellow. The outer surface with the fruit-bearing layer has
longitudinal, separated, vein-like wrinkles with cross-veins which
form a network. It is violet- to grey-brown. The flesh is white, thick,
and soft with a pleasant smell and a mild taste.

It grows in bushes and grass in deciduous and conifer woods from
August to October. It is an excellent edible fungus and can hardly be
confused with any other. Though abundant in the lake districts of
Bavaria and in other alpine districts this fungus is rare in Great Britain.

46. BOLETUS EDULIS

French: CEPE DE BORDEAUX.
Italian: PORCINO.
Spanish: BOLETO COMESTIBLE.   **Edible**
German: STEINPILZ.   Plates 46 and 47, facing p 74

47. RED-CAPPED VARIETY: *var. fuscoruber.*

CAP

TUBES

SPORES

STEM

The *Boletus edulis* is usually fairly large and can become very large
in sheltered places. The cap is 8–20 (30) cm. wide, at first spherical,
later bulging to flattened-convex, the surface smooth, though sometimes wrinkled, usually dry, slightly clammy when moist. The
colour is at first whitish, then grey to light-brown, then red-brown
or chestnut-brown, sometimes darker in the centre with a lighter
margin; when young often showing white striations (cystidia). The
skin of the cap does not peel. The tubes are almost free, at first whitish,
then yellow to yellow-green or dark olive-green and fairly easily
separated from the cap. The tube openings are at first pin-size and
later larger. The spores are olive-brown, spindle-shaped, 12–18μ long.
The flesh is thick, firm and compact, remaining white and only when
old becoming spongy with red zones under the skin of the cap. The
smell is pleasantly fruity, the taste mild and nutty. The vigorous stem,
depending on age, is bulging or cylindrical to club-shaped, often
thicker at the base, streaked with white or fawny-brown when young
with a coarse white network at the top, smooth at the base.

The *Boletus edulis* is one of the best known and sought-after fungi
on account of its excellent flavour, its white flesh, and the fact that it
keeps well. It can be cooked in any way and is easily dried. Unfortunately caterpillars and beetles like it as much as human beings. It is
common in deciduous and conifer woods, at the edges of woods and
on woodland paths, especially under birches. Since it is a micorrhiza
fungus it can grow on the most varied soil and occurs in one or two
sub-species.

One of these, the *Boletus subspec. reticulatus* has a light, pale, grey-
yellow or brownish cap which is slightly downy and often torn and
an equally pale stem with a network of striations down to its base.
This is found from as early as May until July, often abundantly, under
oaks and beeches. It has white soft flesh, brownish under the cap,
with a pleasant smell and a mild pleasant taste and is especially good
for drying.

Another variety, the *Boletus aereus* has a black or dark hemi-spherical cap. It is firm-fleshed, downy, and noticeably chocolate to black brown, velvety and dry, the upper surface like glove leather, and often spotted brick-red to blood-red. Its stem is noticeably bulging and only the upper portion has a network of fine red-brown striations. The tubes are pale yellow to olive-yellow, the spores light yellow-green, 12–15μ long and club shaped. The flesh is fairly tough, quite white, and only grey-brown or red-brown under the skin of the cap. It grows in deciduous woods, especially under oaks, is fairly rare, and an excellent edible fungus.

The yellow variety, *Boletus appendiculatus*, is called the aerus by several writers. Its cap is light- to dark-brown, the tubes, stem and flesh are lemon- to chrome-yellow. The flesh sometimes turns more-or-less blue but sometimes remains unchanged. The spores are 10–16μ long. The base of the stem usually shows definite roots. It is found in deciduous and conifer woods, especially in mountainous regions, is sometimes very large, and is also good to eat.

The red-capped variety–*var. fuscoruber*–has a very large purple-brown to copper-red cap often streaked with violet (with large numbers of cystidia) and is slimy when old, the pores then being tinged rusty-brown. The stem is saffron- to fox-brown, the flesh very firm and white, and wine-red only under the skin of the cap. It grows in Summer and Autumn and is the type of Boletus most often found among firs and in mountain woods. It is a good edible fungus.

The Boletus most often found in pinewoods, the *Boletus pinicola*, has a copper-brown to purple-brown cap which is dry to clammy. It is similar to the foregoing but its margin is often streaked yellow-green, its tubes are at first white, then yellow to light olive-yellow, 12–19μ long, and narrow-elliptical. The stem is usually swollen, white or yellow-brown to red-brown or wine-red, and marked with a more-or-less noticeable net-pattern. The tubes are adnate and light-yellow. The flesh is white, soft and watery with wine-red zones under the skin of the cap. The cap is toned pink or lemon-yellow. It turns grey-yellow when cooked. It has a savoury smell and a mild, pleasant taste. It grows from (May) June to October in deciduous and conifer woods, especially at the base of trees. It is rare, but edible and excellent.

When young all Boleti can be confused with the bitter and inedible *Boletus felleus* (48).

As well as being greatly prized in France, Germany and Italy as one of the best edible fungi, it is the *Boletus edulis* which is used to make the various brands of dehydrated mushroom soup. Translator's note.

48. BOLETUS (TYLOPILUS) FELLEUS

Caution

Plate 48, between pp 74 and 75

CAP This medium-sized fungus is the same shape as the *Boletus edulis*. The cap is 7–12 cm. wide, thick-fleshed, domed to flattened, leather-brown or grey-brown to chestnut or red-brown, more-or-less felty when young, quite smooth when old. The skin does not peel. The TUBES tubes are adnate to free, bulging downwards. When young the spores are very crowded, whitish to rust-brown, when old, more distant, STEM reddish to dull-pink. The stem is dirty-white to olive- or yellow-brown, stout, at first swollen, then more-or-less cylindrical and SPORES covered with a pronounced, wide-meshed network. The spores are spindle-shaped, 12–15μ long, almost colourless. The spore dust is pinkish red. The flesh is white, pinkish when broken or cut, firm when young, spongy and reddish to brown when old. There is little smell. The taste is extremely bitter. This fungus is seldom maggoty, but completely inedible.

It appears in the Autumn, though sometimes earlier from (June) August to October (November), especially in wet years, growing in quantities in conifer woods under firs and pines and keeping to the same habitats. In dry years it may hardly appear at all.

It can only be confused when young with the *Boletus edulis* which it then deceptively resembles but when large it is not difficult to recognise. Cap and stem are almost always olive- to yellow-brown and the pinkish-red to flesh-coloured tubes bulge deeply under the edge of the cap. Tasting a small piece, or even licking a freshly-cut surface is, with its intensely bitter taste, sufficient to identify it.

According to reports from France, Rumania and East Germany it can be eaten after stewing in skimmed milk, and can be used for flavouring when powdered. However, a single specimen, cooked unawares with other fungi, can completely ruin a dish. Although entirely unpalatable it is not considered poisonous.

49. BOLETUS BADIUS

French: BOLET BAI

German:　　　　　　　　　　　**Edible**

　MARONEN-RÖHRLING　　　Plate 49, between pp 74 and 75

CAP This fungus is usually small to medium-sized. The cap is chestnut to chocolate-brown, sometimes almost black-brown, at first globular, then rounded to flattened, 5–15 cm. wide, usually with sharp edges. When young and dry it is finely-felted; old, or in wet weather it is TUBES slightly clammy. The tubes are adnate to free, pale-yellow to yellow-green, usually short and easily detached from the flesh of the cap. The

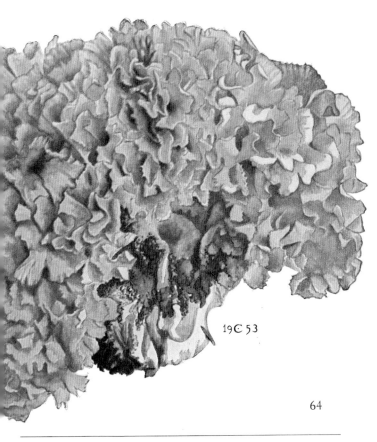

19C 53

64

64. *Sparassis crispa* p 108

65

65. THE COMMON EARTH BALL,
Scleroderma aurantium (vulgare) p 109

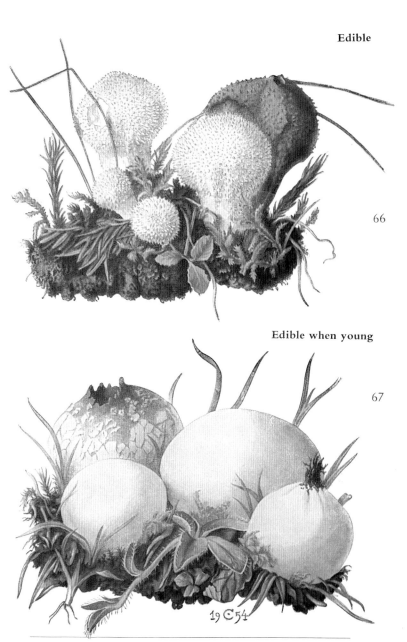

Edible

66

Edible when young

67

66. THE COMMON PUFF BALL,
Lycoperdon perlatum (gemmatum) (upper) p 109
67. *Bovista negrescens* (lower) p 110

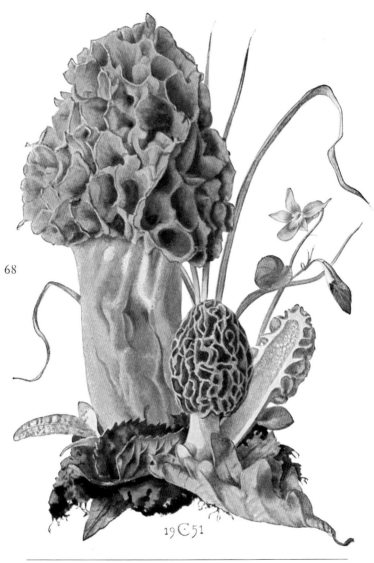

68

68. THE MOREL, *Morchella esculenta* p 111

pores are white to yellow-green, rounded or angular, and become more-or-less blue green when bruised. The spore dust is olive-brown, the spores 15–17μ long. The stem is yellow-brown, 6–12 cm. long, stout, smooth, bulging or cylindrical, longitudinally striated, sometimes with a whitish network, often curved. The flesh is white or pale yellow, firm when young, fibrous in the stem, and becoming more-or-less blue when cut. The smell is fruity, the taste mild and pleasant. The *Boletus badius* is an excellent edible fungus and equal in flavour to the *Boletus edulis*. SPORES
STEM

It grows abundantly from (June) August to November almost everywhere in conifer woods, less frequently in deciduous woods, singly or in clusters, especially at the roots of firs or pines, also in grass and moss at the edges of woods and on hills among the dry pine needles. It often closely resembles the *Boletus edulis* but is usually smaller.

In fact there are two forms of *Boletus badius*, depending on habitat but nevertheless appearing close together. One grows among damp grass or moss and one among dry pine needles. Normally only the first of these is illustrated. This grows in thick moss or among grass in woods, is usually large with a long stem, is always sticky and soft-fleshed, has longer tubes, and often colours a deep blue. When picked, mature specimens, like the *Boletus scaber* (58) often result in an un-attractively-coloured, wet, pulpy mass and are therefore not suitable for collecting. The second form, which grows on dry pine needles is shown characteristically on Plate 49 (below and left). This is usually smaller than the grass and moss type, is always dry, and has short tubes. It is little affected by bruising and hardly turns blue. It often grows in small colonies, has a short, stout stem and is extremely like a small *Boletus edulis*. It is solid and firm, is always in good condition, and so is well worth collecting. The *Boletus badius* can only be confused with similar edible Boleti which are described on the following pages.

50. BOLETUS SUBTOMENTOSUS

Edible

German: ZIEGENLIPPE   Plate 50, facing p 75 (upper)

This fungus is usually no more than medium-sized. The cap is 5–12 (17) cm. wide, hemispherical, then convex to flattened, the surface somewhat downy. The colour is extremely varied, olive-yellow to grey-yellow, dark olive-brown to brown. When old or dry the surface is cracked and torn. The skin does not peel. When young the tubes are bright lemon- to golden-yellow, when old, a dirty yellow-green. They are practically unaffected by bruising, so CAP

TUBES

the colour does not change; almost free at the stem, unequal in
length, with broad angular pores easily detached from the flesh of
SPORES the cap. The spores are spindle-shaped, 10–15μ long. The stem is
STEM 6–11 cm. in length, usually of even thickness, often curved, yellow to
brown, more rarely finely-striated or scaly, almost like a network,
solid and soon becoming woody, tapering towards the base. The
flesh is soft, white or yellow-white, somewhat brown under the skin
of the cap, only occasionaly turning slightly blue. Smell and taste are
fruity, mild and pleasant.

It grows in deciduous and conifer woods, especially among moss
neaɪ the edges of woods, and on grassy paths from June to October
(November), usually singly but quite abundantly. It is an excellent
edible fungus but will not keep long because of its soft flesh.

It can easily be distinguished from the *Boletus chrysenteron* (51),
which is very affected by bruising and turns a dirty blueish-green,
because its tubes are not so affected. The strongly scented *Boletus
fragrans*, with purple-red, usually deeply-inturned margin is probably
merely another form of *Boletus submentosus*. The illustration shows
the very variable appearance of this fungus.

51. BOLETUS CHRYSENTERON

Edible

Plate 51, facing p 75 (lower)

CAP This fungus is usually smaller than the *Boletus submentosus* to which it
is closely related. The cap is 3–8 (10) cm. wide, the colour extremely
varied. The surface is finely-felted or downy, green- or grey-brown
to dark olive, sometimes almost black-green, or again, ochre-grey. It
is cracked into patches from the beginning showing red or purple-red
TUBES between the cracks. The tubes are adnate or adnexed, greeny-yellow
to olive-yellow, very sensitive to bruising and turning blue at once,
SPORES with wide angular pores. The spores are light olive-brown, 10–15μ
STEM long, and spindle shaped. The stem is 3–6 (8) cm. long, usually
slender and even, turning blue when bruised, bright golden-yellow
with streaks of cherry red, with a tapering bright-yellow base. The
flesh is soft, yellow, pale-yellow in the cap, and purple-red under the
skin. Over the tubes it sometimes turns blue when broken or cut. At
the base of the stem it is dull purple-red. The smell is fruity, the taste
mild and pleasant.

It is very common in deciduous and conifer woods from June to
November, always growing in colonies and sometimes very
abundantly, especially on moss or grass near woods. It is an excellent
edible fungus but being soft does not keep well. Unfortunately it is
frequently maggoty, or spoilt by a mildew-like parasitic fungus
(Hypomyces chrysospermas) around the tubes rendering it inedible.

There is no danger in confusing this with other similar fungi since these are all edible, including the *Boletus rubellus* with bright red, sometimes dull pink, velvety cap. The stem of this is usually striated with red fibres. The three types of Boleti; *B. badius*, *B. submentosus*, and *B. chrysenteron* are in practice not always easily distinguished from one another. There seem to be several transitional types for which no classification has been attempted.

52. BOLETUS LUTEUS

Edible

German: BUTTER-RÖHRLING   Plate 52, facing p 82

This is a medium-sized fungus. The cap is 4–10 (13) cm. wide, thick   CAP
fleshed, hemispherical to domed, finally flattened, often umbonate.
In wet weather, and in the early morning it glistens with a brown,
slimy coating. When young the edges are inturned and there is often
a white-skinned and darker veil between the edge of the cap and the   VEIL
top of the stem. The skin of the cap is chocolate-brown, more rarely
yellow-brown with darker patches, shiny in dry weather, and peels
completely. The lemon tubes are adnate, do not change colour, and   TUBES
are easily removable. The pores are narrow, white to lemon-yellow.
The spore dust is olive brown, the spores light yellow to yellow-
brown, 7–11µ long, elliptical. The stem is 3–8 (11) cm. long, stout,   TUBES
of even thickness, often curved, with a large, spreading, white to
violet, membranous and evanescent ring. Above the ring the stem   SPORES
is yellow, with a net pattern and conical white, soon becoming dark   STEM
red-brown, warts which, under the microscope, are seen as clusters
of cystidia. The base of the cap is flecked with brown. The flesh is   RING
thick, soft and delicate, white-yellow to lemon-yellow soon becoming
spongy. At the base of the stem it is red and soon becomes rotten.
There is a fruity smell, the taste is mild and pleasantly sharp.

It grows in conifer woods, especially among pines, at the edges of
woods and on grassy banks from Summer to late Autumn, often in
colonies and sometimes very abundantly. It is an excellent edible
fungus, well-suited to frying, but it will not keep and is not suitable
for drying. The slimy skin should be removed when this fungus is
collected in order to avoid spoiling other fungi you have picked. It can
be confused–though quite harmlessly–with the *Boletus granulatus* (53).

53. BOLETUS GRANULATUS

Edible

Plate 53, between pp 82 and 83

This fungus is small to medium-sized. The cap is 2–8 (14) cm. wide,   CAP
hemispherical to convex, the edge at first inrolled, yellow-brown to

leather-brown or straw-yellow, at first slimy, smooth and glistening when dry. The skin peels easily. The tubes are short, light lemon- to olive yellow, medium-sized, adnate, easily detached from the flesh of the cap. The pores are yellow to olive-yellow, rounded angular. When young they exude white, bitter, milky drops. The spore dust is olive-brown, the spores yellow, 8–11μ long, spindle-shaped. The slender even stem is 4–8 cm long, light lemon-yellow, the apex covered with small white to yellow granules which become purple-brown when dry. The flesh is white to light-yellow, unchanged when bruised. In the stem it is deeper yellow, firm when young, moist and spongy when old. The smell is fruity and the taste mild.

This fungus occurs, in places abundantly, from June to October in deciduous and conifer woods, occasionally also on grass near woods and on pastures. It is a good edible fungus, but must be used immediately and soon becomes maggoty. The slimy skin should be removed when collecting in order to avoid spoiling your other specimens.

54. BOLETUS SATANUS

Poisonous

Plate 54, between pp 82 and 83

CAP   The cap of this large and handsomely-coloured fungus is 6–18 (30) cm. wide, convex to flattened, at first with inrolled margin, and becoming very thick-fleshed and firm, When young it rests on the globular stem rather like a priest's cap. The skin of the cap is at first dirty white or dun, becoming pale-grey to silver-grey or olive-grey and, when old, a faded yellow, always tinged with green. It has a velvet sheen, soft to the touch, will not peel and is sticky in wet

TUBES   weather. The tubes are up to 3 mm. long, slightly adnate to free, at first with yellow to yellow-green narrow rounded pores which soon become carmine to purple-red. The tubes are easily detached from the flesh of the cap and turn greeny-blue when bruised. The spore

SPORES   dust is olive green, the single spores spindle-shaped, olive-yellow,
STEM   10–16μ long. The stem is usually short and very swollen (up to 10 cm. in diameter) lemon-yellow at the apex with a carmine, sometimes bright red or yellow zone in the middle and a fine blood-red network. The flesh is usually white though sometimes, especially when young, yellow. It is firm, but spongy and soft, when old. White-fleshed portions of the skin turn blue only slowly and weakly, like watered ink, the rarer yellow-fleshed portions blue more quickly and a darker shade, while in the stem they become reddish but are pale when the fungus is old or dried.

The smell is unpleasant even in young specimens and, when old, is typical, rather like carrion and very unpleasant indeed. Young specimens have a quite pleasant nutty taste.

Raw it is, even in small quantities decidedly poisonous, causing serious intestinal disorders as well as affecting the heart but there is no record of death resulting. Beginners should study this fungus carefully and, until they can recognise it without fail, avoid all Boleti with red pores. All of these, eaten raw, or insufficiently cooked, can cause serious symptoms of poisoning. See P 42.

55. BOLETUS ERYTHROPUS

Caution

Plate 55, facing p 83 (centre and below)

This is a large, unusually conspicuous, dark-toned fungus. The cap is CAP 6–15 (20) cm. wide, hemispherical to convex, solid and thick-fleshed. The skin is finely downy, in places dark-brown to nearly black-brown with an olive-green sheen. It becomes paler and smooth with age, darkens when pressed and does not peel. The tubes are sinuate TUBES and bulge downwards when old. They are at first yellow-green with golden-yellow to olive-red, becoming dull-red to blood-red pores which immediately turn blue-black when bruised or cut. The spore SPORES dust is olive green, the spores yellow-green, spindle-shaped, 11–19μ long. The stem is 4–12 cm. long, sturdy, bulging or evenly thick, STEM basically yellow, stippled with orange-red to carmine red scales or fibrils. There is no network. When old the colour is basically brown-red, immediately turning blue when bruised. The flesh remains firm and compact, bright sulphur- or lemon-yellow turning blue to dark blue when cut or broken, and becoming paler and somewhat ochre-yellow when kept for some time or when cooked. The flesh of the stem is saffron-yellow and at the base more or less red. There is little smell. The taste is mild and somewhat acid.

This fungus grows from May to November singly but fairly abundantly in deciduous and conifer woods, especially under beeches and firs, on chalk-free acid soil often in the same places as the *Boletus edulis*. It hardly ever becomes maggoty and is a good edible fungus though it can cause gastric disorders when raw. It should therefore be well cooked and should be avoided by those with weak digestions.

It can be confused with other edible Boleti, but also with the poisonous *Boletus satanus* (54), though this always has a pale cap, usually whitish flesh and colours light blue when bruised (young specimens can have yellower flesh and colour a darker blue.) Until the various red-pored Boleti are thoroughly known it is better not to eat them. (See p. 42.)

56. BOLETUS LURIDUS

Caution

Plate 56, facing p 83 (upper)

CAP

This large and fine looking fungus very closely resembles the *Boletus erythropus*. The cap is 6–15 (20) cm. wide and convex. The colour varies considerably from dull olive-yellow, brown or red-brown to dark olive-brown. The surface is finely felted with the feel of soft leather. It is sticky in wet weather, smooth and dry when old. The

TUBES

tubes are almost free, fairly long, yellow to yellow-green. The pores are olive-yellow to orange-red becoming dull red-brown to yellow-green when old. Where bruised the surface immediately colours dark

SPORES

blue-green. The base of the tubes is more-or-less red. The spores are

STEM

yellowish, egg- to spindle-shaped, 9–17μ long. The stem is at first bulging, later long and uniformly thick, bright yellow to orange-red. At the base it tapers and is dark purple, almost blackish-red. There is always a prominent, broad-meshed network pattern and a number of felty dots. The flesh is mainly pale yellow, sometimes bright yellow, with wine-red streaks in the cap and the top of the stem, and dark red at the base of the stem. It colours a deep blue when broken or cut, There is little smell and the taste is mild.

This fungus grows from July to October (November) in deciduous and conifer woods and also in parks, especially on chalky soil, often profusely. Eaten raw or insufficiently cooked or with alcohol it has a poisonous effect and causes gastric disorders. Although well flavoured when cooked it can only be described with qualifications as edible.

It is sometimes mistaken for the *Boletus satanus* and can also be confused with the *Boletus erythropus*.

57. BOLETUS CALOPUS

Caution

Plate 57, facing p 90

CAP

This fungus is quite large. The cap is 6–15 (20) cm. wide, sturdy and thick-fleshed, globular with an inrolled margin, then convex, pale grey to olive, or dun to grey-yellow, smooth, downy, with the feel

TUBES

of soft leather. The tubes are round and wide, medium long, almost free, difficult to detach, with very fine lemon- to sulphur-yellow or olive yellow-green pores which at once turn blue-green when

SPORES

bruised. The spore dust is dark olive brown, the spores elliptical spindle-

STEM

shaped, smooth, pale yellow-brown, 10–14μ long. The stem is bulging to elongated, 5–7 cm. long, firm and solid, mainly yellow at the apex, below a fine carmine to dark red with a marked reddish or

yellow-white network. It colours dull green to black when bruised.
The flesh is firm, pale-yellow; pale blue when the cap is cut, and blue
at the base of the tubes. There is a sour, unpleasant smell. The taste
is usually very bitter.

This fungus is common in deciduous and conifer woods, especially
under beeches, usually growing in colonies, from July to October.
Its bitterness makes it quite inedible and slightly poisonous.

It is closely resembled by the more rare *Boletus radicans (=albidus)*
as well as by the poisonous *Boletus satanus* (54). It is sometimes
confused with the *Boletus edulis* but can be distinguished from this by
the red on its stem and by its bitterness. The lemon-yellow tubes,
different smell and bitter taste distinguish it from the *Boletus erythropus*.

58. BOLETUS SCABER

French: BOLET RUDE   **Edible**
German: BIRKEN-RÖHRLING   Plate 58, between pp 90 and 91 (left)

This is a medium-sized fungus. The cap is 5–10 (12) cm. wide hemi-   CAP
spherical to convex, at first firm and dry, then soft-fleshed, usually
smooth but sometimes wrinkled, sticky in early morning and in wet
weather. The colour is light-brown to dark grey-brown, pale-grey
or dark-brown, sometimes almost white. The tubes are adnate or   TUBES
almost free, very long, bulging below and easily detached from the cap,
with whitish, then dirty-grey, small, round, narrow pores which colour
brown when bruised. The spores are pale-yellow, spindle-shaped,   SPORES
13–20µ long. The stem is up to 15 cm. long, solid either tapering   STEM
towards the apex or evenly thick, sometimes expanded at the base. Its
surface is rough, with small black scales and fibres on a white base. The
flesh is soft, white or grey, soon becoming moist and spongy, very
moist in rain, fibrous and tough when old. Taste and smell are pleasant.

It is common in woods, especially near birches, from June to
October, usually singly but sometimes growing abundantly. When
young it is a very good, soft-fleshed, tasty edible fungus. Old it soon
becomes spongy, slimy, and unattractive. It should be used quickly
and is good for soups, stews, or as a vegetable. It can be dried.

It can be confused with other rare, edible species growing near
birch trees.

59. BOLETUS AURANTIACUS and
BOLETUS TESTACEOSCABER (VERSIPELLIS)
formerly: *Boletus versipellis*

Edible
Plate 59, between pp 90 and 91 (right)

These are medium to large fungi, brightly coloured. The caps are   CAP
7–20 cm. wide, hemispherical to convex, sometimes also flattened,

and always thick-fleshed and robust. *Boletus aurantiacus* is dark red-brown to orange red-brown. *Boletus testaceoscaber* is somewhat lighter, orange-yellow to yellow-brown, often with flabby membranous remains from the edge of the cap stretching like a veil

TUBES   towards the tubes. The tubes are free. *Boletus aurantiacus* has whitish pores. *Boletus testaceoscaber* has, from youth onwards, grey to dark-

SPORES   grey or rust-brown pores. The spores are brown, spindle-shaped,

STEMS   10–16 (18)μ long. The stems are 10–15 cm. long, very sturdy and compressed, narrowing towards the apex, and white. The stem of *Boletus aurantiacus* has white to red-brown fibrous scales. On *Boletus testaceoscaber* these are blackish. The flesh is firm becoming soft. **In** *Boletus aurantiacus* it is white, then lilac to blackish, in *Boletus testaceoscaber* it is white, then pink to lilac, colouring blue to greenish in the stem. When cooked it turns black. Smell and taste are pleasant and mild.

     Boletus testaceoscaber is found mainly in conifer and birch woods. *Boletus aurantiacus* grows in deciduous woods and on heaths, especially under birches, also under aspen. It is much less common then *Boletus testaceoscaber*. Both species are common from June to October. They are both good, edible fungi, and can also be pickled or dried. When young, when the caps are still small and the stems have already shot up, they look very like large matches. They can only be confused with edible Boleti.

60. SARCODON (HYDNUM) IMBRICATUM

Edible

Plate 60, between pp 90 and 91 (upper)

CAP   The cap of this medium to large fungus is 5–20 (25) cm. wide, at first somewhat inturned, depressed to concave in the centre, chocolate-brown with darker, large, circular, tile-like scales resembling a hawk's

SPINES   plumage. On the lower surface of the cap are 'teeth' or spines, 8–12 mm. long, thickset and decurrent, whitish-grey to grey-

SPORES   brown, dark-brown when old and very fragile. The spores are

STEM   rounded, brown, spiny, 6–7μ long. The stem is 3–6 cm. thick, grey-white to pale brown, solid, smooth, slightly felted at the base. The flesh is firm, dirty-white to grey-brown with a pleasant spice-like smell and a mild taste, often bitter when old.

     It is common in sandy conifer woods, especially among pines, from August to November, particularly in hill districts. When young it is a good edible fungus with an excellent, strong flavour, especially good for flavouring. In wet weather, and when old, it is often tough, bitter and maggoty. It can be bottled, or dried and pulverised to be used for flavouring.

     It can only be confused with the very bitter *Sarcodon (scabrosum) amarescans* although the stem of this is blue-black. This fungus is so bitter as to be completely inedible and it is very rare.

69

69. *Gyromitra (Helvella) esculenta* p 112

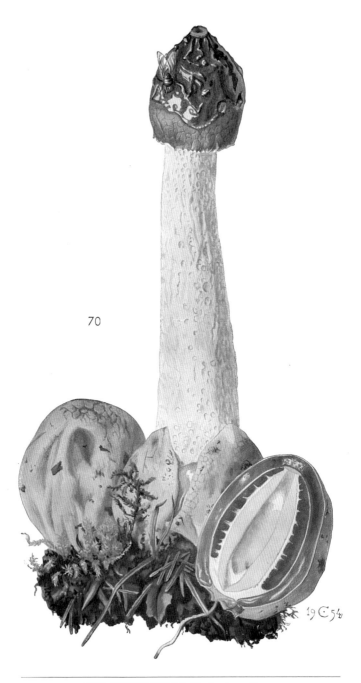

70

70. THE STINKHORN, *Phallus impudicus* p 113

61. HYDNUM (SARCODON) REPANDUM

French: PIED DE MOUTON   **Edible**
German: SEMMELPILZ   Plate 61, between pp 90 and 91 (lower)
Italian: GALLINACCIO SPINOSO

This fungus is small to medium-sized. The cap is irregularly shaped,   CAP
5–12 (20) cm. wide, full-fleshed, with irregularly-undulating curves,
then flattened-convex, pale-yellow to egg-yellow or darker yellow
to pale red. The skin of the cap is dry and often cracked. The spines   SPINES
are fairly thickset, unequal in length, decurrent, pale yellow to flesh-
coloured, and very fragile. The spore dust is translucent. The spores   SPORES
are white, rounded, smooth, 8–9µ long. The stem is short, up to 6 cm.   STEM
long, often eccentric, thick and whitish. The flesh is compact, fragile,
white to yellow. The smell is pleasant and the taste mild, though
bitter when old.

It grows in deciduous and conifer woods, sometimes abundantly,
from July to November. Young it is excellent to eat and seldom
maggoty. The slight bitterness disappears on cooking.

From above it is often deceptively like the Chanterelle. Resembling
it is the, also edible, *Hydnum rufescens*, which is never bitter, as well
as the, usually bitter and so inedible, *Polyporus confluens* (without spines).

62. CLAVARIA (RAMARIA) AUREA

                                        Edible when young
[1]*German:* GOLDGELBE KORALLE   Plate 62, facing p 91 (upper)

The medium-sized fruit-body or sporophore is roughly spherical,   SHAPE
branched like a cauliflower, 6–12 (16) cm. high, and about the same
diameter. It develops from a pale (soon becoming light yellow)
elastic stalk, 3–4 cm. thick which divides into numerous forked   STALK
branches. These are compact and firm, pointing upwards, and ending
in blunt, bifurcating, teeth-like tips. The whitish, watery flesh is
brittle, marbled, with a pleasant, rather sour smell and a mild taste.
The spore dust is yellow, the spores pale yellow, cylindrical and   SPORES
rough, 9–10µ long.

This fungus occurs in deciduous and conifer woods from Summer
to Autumn, singly and in clusters, as well as in rows and rings. It is
only edible when young. When old it is very fibrous and tough and
can only be used to flavour soups or sauces, while really old specimens
can cause ill effects. Dried it can only be used for flavouring.

This fungus can only be confused with the lemon-yellow *Clavaria
(Ramaria) flava* which is edible and good.

---

[1] The German edition of this book lists, among others, no fewer than twenty-
six different German folk-names for this fungus! Translator's Note.

H

63. CLAVARIA (RAMARIA) PALLIDA

Poisonous
Plate 63, facing p 91 (lower)

STALK
SPORES

The medium-sized fruit-body grows to a height of 7–10 (12) cm. There are numerous branches, dull yellow, dull yellow-brown or flesh-coloured to café-au-lait forking from a fairly thick, short, pale grey-yellow stalk which is whitish at the base. The tips are mostly a lilac-violet colour when young. The spores are yellowish, egg-shaped, 9–12μ long. The flesh is white, firm and dry. This fungus has a somewhat tart, slightly soapy smell and a bitter taste when raw. It is also unpleasantly bitter and acid when cooked.

It grows mostly on chalky soil in beechwoods, but also in conifer woods, sometimes abundantly, from August to early October. Although not deadly poisonous it must be regarded as dangerous since it can cause serious gastric disorder with pain, sickness and diarrhoea. It is claimed that if the branching tips are cut off the rest is edible and harmless but this seems very doubtful.

Similar in appearance and in its effects is the poisonous *Clavaria (Ramaria) formosa*. This grows to a height of 20 cm., has a whitish stalk, pink in the centre with yellow branches and yellow tips. The flesh is white, with an unpleasant taste and smell. The colour and taste are sufficient to distinguish it. Beginners should avoid all grey-yellow or brownish-red, and bitter specimens of Clavaria, as well as all old specimens. See p 44.

64. SPARASSIS CRISPA

Italian: SPUGNOLA D'AUTUNNO CRESPA　　**Edible**
German: KRAUSE GLUCKE　　Plate 64, between pp 98 and 99

SHAPE
STALK
SPORES

This fungus is rounded and looks rather like a sponge. It can be the size of a clenched fist or of a human head, averaging 15–30 cm. across, though giant specimens do occur. The stalk is thick-fleshed, growing deep in the ground. Growing out of this is a mass of dense branches, flattened, wavy and twisted, with whitish and pale-yellow ends, the edges brownish when old. The spores are broadly elliptical, smooth, colourless to pale-yellow, 6–7μ long. The flesh is white, with a pleasant aromatic smell when young, and a mild, nutty taste. Fresh or dried it is a good edible fungus, excellent fried with eggs, or fried in batter. It needs thorough washing to remove dirt or insects. When old it is tough and bitter and cannot be eaten. Spongy or brown portions should be cut away since these can cause serious gastric trouble. It can be dried, powdered, and used for flavouring.

It is not uncommon in Autumn, growing on the ground in conifer woods from July to October (November) on or near stumps of pine. Very similar to it is the equally large *Sparassis laminosa* with very wide, ribbon-like, flat branches. This is also edible and good. It grows at the same time of the year in deciduous woods, especially under oaks.

65. THE COMMON EARTH BALL
Scleroderma aurantium, (vulgare)

Caution

German: KARTOFFEL BOVIST Plate 65, between pp 98 and 99

The fruit-body is more-or-less potato-shaped, firm, hard, flattened- SHAPE bulbous or globular with almost no stem, attached to the ground by a rootlike mass of white, bushy mycelium threads. The outer skin (peridium) is 1.5–3 mm. thick, fleshy, or tough as leather, or again cork-like, dry and hard, becoming covered on the upper surface with wart-like or scaly protruberances, although this may sometimes remain almost smooth. The colour is whitish-yellow to ochre or brownish, the warts being darker. When ripe, it bursts irregularly. The inner fruit mass, the *Gleba* is first fleshy, greenish- to yellowish-white becoming pinkish when cut, soon becoming grey-blue to violet-black, black when ripe, and olive-grey when old. It is traversed by whitish, fibrous veins. Under the microscope pear-shaped basidiae, each with four globular spores, can be seen. When ripe the SPORES interior becomes a blackish-brown mass of spore dust. The spores are rounded and spiny, black-brown, 8–12μ long. There is a strong, acrid, aromatic but unpleasant smell and the taste is acrid.

The Earth Ball is common in woods, on heaths and woodland paths from July to November, growing abundantly in places and keeping to the same habitats. Eaten raw it is poisonous, especially when mature. Even cooked, it causes gastric disorder if eaten in any quantity. It is sometimes mistaken for a truffle. See pp 42 and 43.

66. THE COMMON PUFF BALL
Lycoperdon perlatum (gemmatum)

French: VESSE DE LOUP **Edible**
German: Plate 66, between pp 98 and 99 (upper)
FLASCHEN-STÄUBLING

The size of the fruit-body varies considerably. It is flask- or pear- SHAPE shaped, the upper part being globular with a cylindrical stem below, 3–8 (10) cm. high and 3–5 cm. across. The double-skinned outer layer is at first white, then yellowish. The rounded upper surface is covered with dense, fragile spines which easily fall off or rub off, and cone-shaped warts. When mature it becomes brownish, paper-thin, smooth, and bursts at the top through a small round opening. At this stage the slightest touch releases a cloud of olive-brown spore dust. The spore-forming inner flesh – the *Gleba* – is white when young, becoming yellow- to olive brown. When mature it is a dry dust, becoming grey-brown with age. The spores are rounded, short-stemmed, slightly warty, light olive-brown, 3.5–4μ long. There is a strong radish-like smell which disappears with cooking. The taste is mild.

SPORES

This is the commonest of all the puff-balls, growing abundantly in woods, pastures, and other grassy places from June to November. When young, while the flesh is still white, it is excellent to eat and is especially good fried. All puff-balls should be used immediately since they can mature after picking and are then useless. They should be peeled not washed, and are excellent fried in batter. The white forms of the puff-ball can hardly be confused with other fungi or, at the most, with other forms of puff-ball, since there are numerous varieties, difficult to distinguish without a microscope.

67. BOVISTA NEGRESCENS
Edible when young
Plate 67, between pp 98 and 99 (lower)

SHAPE

The small fruit-body is globular, without a stem, usually wider than it is high, white and smooth. It grows to the size of an egg and is attached to the ground by strands of mycelium. The outer covering (Peridium) is white, and consists of two layers. When mature, the outer layer cracks and peels off in scale-like flakes. The paper-thin, tough and permanent inner skin is at first white to yellow, or grey-brown and shining becoming dark-brown to black. It bursts at the top leaving a small, irregularly-torn opening through which the spore dust is expelled at the slightest touch. The inner flesh is at first marrow-like and white. It then becomes soft and bright yellow or yellow brown to olive-brown. When mature it is purple to black-brown and finally becomes dry and dusty. The spore dust is olive-brown to purple-brown. The spores are spherical, stemmed, 5–6μ long. There is a somewhat fruitlike smell and, when raw, almost no taste. When young, while the flesh is still white, it is edible and good. It should be peeled before cooking.

SPORES

It grows in grass, sometimes in clusters, occuring in pastures and meadows and on downs and heaths from June to November. In the Autumn it becomes detached from the ground and is often blown about by the wind.

Very similar but smaller is the Dwarf puff-ball, *Bovista plumbea*. The inner skin of this becomes blue-grey when mature. It grows in the same places and is also edible. Also frequently found in the same habitats is the Giant Puff-ball, *Lycoperdon (Calvatia) giganteum* which often grows to a foot or more in diameter. This is also edible, and excellent when young. Like all the puff-balls it should be peeled before cooking.

68. THE MOREL
Morchella esculenta

French: MORILLE.
Italian: SPUGNOLA ESCULENTA   **Edible**
German: SPEISEMORCHEL   Plate 68, between pp 98 and 99

The distinctive cap varies considerably in colour and shape. It may be   CAP
globular, or egg-shaped to conical, and more-or-less curved, 3–7 cm.
high and 3–5 cm. across, and giant specimens do sometimes occur.
The surface is divided into a honeycomb-like network by deep ridges
and lateral folds or ribs forming deep, irregular, cell-like pits. The
colour is light ochre to deep brown, sometimes whitish-grey to dark
grey, the edges of the ridges being black when old. The spores are   SPORES
smooth, rounded-elliptical, 16–23μ long, colourless to pale yellow.
The stem is 3–10 cm. high, thick and furrowed, but thin-fleshed and   STEM
hollow, frequently thicker at the base, in colour white to pale yellow.
The flesh is white, wax-like and brittle, with a pleasantly aromatic
taste and smell.

The Morel favours chalky soil, also places where there have been
fires, and grows near trees, especially under elm, ash, and poplar, but
also in parks and among bushes, as well as in mountainous districts. It
occurs in April and May, especially after rain, and recurs in the same
places. During the last war it was frequently found growing among
the ruins. The Morel is edible and excellent to eat, and generally a
much sought-after delicacy, though it is said to be indigestible if
eaten in quantity. Dried and ground to powder it is excellent for
flavouring.

68a MORCHELLA CONICA

Edible
Not illustrated

The medium-sized cap is narrow, egg-shaped to conical. 7–10 cm.   CAP
high, and 4 cm. across, with almost-straight, rectangular, honeycomb-
like pits with prominent vertical ribs and less-prominent horizontal
divisions. It is hollow and fragile, olive-brown to olive-black and
blackish at the edges of the ribs. The stem is usually equal in length to   STEM
the cap, hollow and brittle, whitish, smooth and mealy. The spores   SPERES
are elliptical, colourless, 18–25μ long. The flesh is waxy and brittle.

This fungus favours chalky or sandy soil and occurs in woods and gardens, on damp meadows, and especially where anything has been burned, in April and May. It is edible and good, especially when young and can also be dried, powdered, and used for flavouring. Old specimens, often mildewed, can be dangerous. Elongated, pointed specimens of the *Morchella esculenta* are often confused with this fungus.

Very similar is the *Morchella elata*, 4–7 cm. long, with light-brown to olive-brown, elongated and conical cap, prominent vertical, and less-prominent horizontal divisions. Its stem is at least 4 cm. long, cylindrical, whitish to ochre, often twisted vertically, mealy and thickened at the base. This also occurs in woods, among bushes, and on pastures near woods, from April to May and is also a good edible fungus.

69. GYROMITRA (HELVELLA) ESCULENTA

Poisonous
Plate 69, facing p 106

CAP The cap, often fist-size, is very irregular in shape, roughly globular, usually wider than it is high, occasionally divided, with more than one tip. The surface resembles that of a brain, having thick, twisting, irregular folds or convolutions, chestnut to sooty-brown in colour, whitish to grey-white within, joined in places to the stem. The spore
SPORES dust is whitish, the spores transparent, elliptical, 17–22μ long. The
STEM stem is up to 7 cm. long, usually short and thick, pithy and either showing cavities when cut or hollow, grooved, grey-white in colour and somewhat felted. The flesh is waxy, very thin and brittle. Smell and taste are mild and pleasant.

This fungus grows on sandy soil in conifer woods, especially where there has been a fire, and among dry brushwood, appearing in April and May.

Although formerly believed to be good and edible, numerous cases of poisoning (on the Continent) reveal it to be decidedly dangerous and it is now prohibited from sale in markets in Germany. Eaten raw it is poisonous and even deadly. It can only be eaten if first boiled in water for at least five minutes. The water must be thrown away and the fungus rinsed in fresh water. (The poison, helvellic acid, is soluble in boiling water and is thus, at least in part, removed). However, many people have become ill after eating it, even when prepared in this way, and it is undoubtedly best avoided, though said to be perfectly safe when dried.

Very similar to the *Gyromitra esculenta,* also in its poisonous effect, is the *Gyromitra gigas,* with a pale-yellow to olive-brown cap. This should only be eaten after taking the above-mentioned precaution. See p. 40.

70. THE STINKHORN

Phallus impudicus

German: STINKMORCHEL
Italian: SATIRIONE

Plate 70, facing p 107

Owing to its shape the Stinkhorn might be mistaken for a type of   SHAPE
Morel. However, the Morels, the Helvellas and the Pezizas (Cup
Fungi) belong to the class Ascomycetes (sack fungi, see p. 22) while
the Stinkhorn is a Basidiomycete.

The fruit body of the Stinkhorn begins underground. When it first
appears above ground it is spherical to egg-shaped and enclosed by a
double-walled outer covering (the Primary Peridium or Volva) with
a gelatinous intermediate layer. It is then about the size of an egg, soft
and springy, attached to the ground by rootlike strands of mycelium.
A cross-section at this stage shows a surprisingly varied colour design:
first a tough, white to leather-yellow, outer skin, (the Peridium) and
beneath this an olive-brown, transparent gelatinous layer and a frailer,
white inner layer (the Receptaculum) on the under surface of which
is the olive-green fruit mass (the Gleba), sheathed in white tissue. In
the centre is the white hollow stem. On maturing the stem quickly   STEM
elongates, breaks through the covering layer and emerges with the
'cap', the outside of which is slimy and carries the fruit mass. The stem
is pure white, elastic, slightly pitted, hollow, narrowing above. It
carries at the top the thimble-sized or larger, bell-shaped 'cap', hang-   CAP
ing almost free on the stem, and covered with a shining, olive-green,
jelley-like mass which on maturity drips down as a slimy liquid. This
contains the spores and emits a penetrating and highly-unpleasant
smell which attracts insects, flies and beetles to feed on it. The earlier
egg-shaped covering layer remains like a volva at the base of the stem.
Soon the slimy liquid drips away completely, leaving a pure white,
delicate, almost odourless cap which is in fact a ring corresponding to
the ring of an Amanita, while the olive-green mass is the fruit-body.
The formerly-robust, stem wilts and droops to the ground where it
gradually rots. The various insects it had attracted fly of to the next
Stinkhorn, helping to distribute the spores. The spores are olive-   SPORES
coloured, rod-shaped, only 3–5µ long.

The Stinkhorn is common from June to November in deciduous
and conifer woods as well as in parks and gardens. It is not infrequent
in cemetaries, hence a grim legend in Germany likening it to dead
men's fingers

When mature it is exceedingly unpleasant, quite inedible, and was
formerly thought to be poisonous. When young, in the egg-shaped
form, it is not in the least unpleasant and is actually considered a
delicacy in some parts of Germany where it is also sold in Delikates-
sen shops as a kind of truffle. It is also pickled and used in sausages
which people enjoy in the belief that they are truffled.

In the Middle Ages the Stinkhorn was used for love potions and also—made into an ointment—as a cure for gout.

It can hardly be confused with any other fungus.

Similar but more rare is the *Mutinus caninus*. The stem (receptacle) of this is vermilion, the head olive-green with an ochre-brown volva at the base. The odour of its spore mass is very similar to cats' faeces.

BIBLIOGRAPHY

(*As the original Bibliography naturally refers almost exclusively to German publications, a new one has been prepared for English readers.*)

John Ramsbottom, *A Handbook of the Larger British Fungi*, The British Museum (Natural History), 1951.

John Ramsbottom, *Mushrooms and Toadstools*, Collins, 1954.

John Ramsbottom, *Edible Fungi*, King Penguin, 1948.

John Ramsbottom, *Poisonous Fungi*, King Penguin, 1948.

Elsie M. Wakefield and R. W. G. Dennis, *Common British Fungi*, P. R. Gawthorn Ltd., 1950.

Ministry of Agriculture and Fisheries, *Edible and Poisonous Fungi*, H.M. Stationery Office, 1947.

Morton Lange & F. Bayard Hora, *Collins Guide to Mushrooms and Toadstools*, Collins, 1965.

The following are monographs published by, and obtainable from, The Naturalist, University of Leeds:

A.A. Pearson: *Notes on the Boleti*, July–Sept. 1946 (No. 818) gives a full list of British species.

The Genus Russula, July–Sept. 1948 (No. 826), as above.

The Genus Lactarius, 1950.

G. R. Bisbey, *An Introduction to the Taxonomy and Nomenclature of Fungi*, Imperial Mycological Institute, 1945.

Claire Loewenfeld, *Britain's Wild Larder: FUNGI*, Faber & Faber. (An excellent and comprehensive collection of fungus recipes).

Valentina P. Wasson & R. Gordon Wasson, *Mushrooms, Russia and History*. (A beautiful and brilliant study of the Folklore and History of wild mushrooms. With fine colour-plates. To quote the authors: 'It is the first treatment in any language of the role played by mushrooms in the daily lives of the various European peoples.' A limited, de-luxe edition.)

Robert Graves, *What Food the Centaurs Ate* (Steps: Cassell & Co., 1958). (See pp 319–343 for the suggestion that *Amanita muscaria* was eaten by the Satyrs, Centaurs, and Maenads of Greek Myths. See also the FOREWORD to *The Greek Myths* 1, Robert Graves Penguin Books, 1966.)

John Braun: Advertisements in Court (London, 1965. Distributor: P. M. Associates, 68A, Wigmore Street, London W1). (Chapter 6. entitled 'When is a Mushroom . . .?' examines the 1965 legal case when a manufacturer of canned soup labelled 'Mushroom Soup' was summonsed under the Food and Drugs Acts and alleged to be supplying food for sale not marked with a true statement and had supplied for sale food falsely labelled as mushroom soup.

The manufacturer admitted that what was stated to be dehydrated mushroom was in fact dehydrated spores of *Boletus edulis* and pleaded not guilty. (He won his case).

This case underlines many points of interest to wild mushroom enthusiasts, especially that (1) dehydrated spores of *Boletus edulis* give a more 'mushroom-flavoured' mushroom soup than do what are the only species normally considered by English-speaking peoples to be 'Mushrooms' and so safe (i.e. *Agaricus campestris,* or *Agaricus bisporus)*, (2) that every man, woman and child in the U.K. who may be presumed to have eaten and enjoyed, (and lived after) the ever-popular canned or dehydrated mushroom soups has actually been partaking of one of those 'toadstools' which he has always been taught to regard as deadly, (3) that the word 'toadstool' in any pejorative sense should now presumably be limited to the half-dozen very dangerous species–or disappear.

COOKING FUNGI

by Otto Gregory

(Here it is impossible to give more than a few recipes. A very fine selection of fungus recipes is given in the Penguin Handbook, *Plats du Jour* by Patience Gray and Primrose Boyd. A still larger, collection is to be found in *Britain's Wild Larder·Fungi* by Claire Loewenfeld.)

Preparation

The fungi should be trimmed and inedible or maggoty parts removed. Dirt can usually be removed by wiping with a damp cloth. Some species, however, especially Morels and Chanterelles, need well-washing under the tap. If they are to be fried, they should then be dried as well as possible. Stems should be removed but, unless they are very tough, these may be sliced and cooked with the caps. Unless the skin is very tough fungi do not need peeling. Small and young caps are usually cooked whole; if large, and at all tough, they should be sliced. Except when very young, the tubes of Boleti should be removed as they may give a slimy consistency to the dish. In general fungi should be cooked for the minimum time needed to make them tender. Overcooking, especially frying them too long, makes them tough.

Breakfast

Mushrooms with bacon is a traditional British breakfast dish, and just about all the edible species of fungi are also good fried in bacon fat over a low heat. Blewits, Shaggy Caps (young), Parasol Mushrooms and Ceps *(Boletus edulis)* are especially good fried with bacon.

Equally good for breakfast are fungi, gently simmered until tender in butter with a very little milk, chopped parsley and pepper and salt. Serve on hot buttered toast.

Also good as a breakfast dish are Fungi and Scrambled eggs. The fungi are sliced and simmered in a pan with butter until tender. The seasoned beaten-egg mixture is then poured into the pan, the fungi are stirred into it, and it is then scrambled in the normal way.

Main Meals

On the Continent, in the fungus season, especially in Austria, Germany, Switzerland, Italy, France and Eastern Europe various edible species are sold and are regularly served, at home and in restaurants, as a vegetable accompanying the meat, or alone as a savoury. They are also excellent for soups or stews. A few recipes for main-meal dishes are given here and in these I propose to discard the artificial and slightly-pejorative word 'fungi' in favour of the designation which is gradually coming into use for other varieties as well as the Common Mushroom and call them simply: Wild Mushrooms, or even mushrooms.

WILD MUSHROOM and RICE SOUP (German recipe)

1 lb. Wild mushrooms	1½ ozs. Butter
2 pts. Meat or Vegetable Stock	1½ ozs. Rice
chopped Parsley, Seasoning	

Wash, drain and dry the mushrooms and cut into thin slices. Melt butter in a saucepan and simmer mushrooms in it over gentle heat for about 15 minutes. In the meantime put rice into stock, bring it to the boil and simmer until rice is nearly cooked. Add the mushrooms, correct seasoning, and simmer 2–3 minutes. Add chopped parsley before serving.

WILD MUSHROOM and POTATO SOUP   (German recipe)

1 lb. Wild mushrooms	1 Leek (sliced)
3 ozs. finely-chopped Bacon	2 pts. Stock or Water
1 (sliced) Onion	2 Tablespoonfuls Sour cream
½ lb. Potatoes	

Fry the chopped bacon until the fat has melted and then sweat the sliced onion and sliced leek in the fat. Add the sliced mushrooms and cook these very gently for 5 minutes. Transfer the contents of the pan, together with the sliced potatoes, to a saucepan containing the water or stock and simmer, covered, for about 45 minutes. When the potatoes are soft add the sour cream and season with pepper and salt and, if water was used, perhaps with a little meat extract. Reheat, stirring, and serve with chopped parsley sprinkled over.

WILD MUSHROOM SALADS
Raw Salads
All edible species of wild mushroom which are not expressly stated
to be poisonous when raw, are excellent raw and sliced in salads. The
mushrooms should be trimmed, well washed under the tap, dried,
and then finely sliced. They are then put into a bowl and seasoned
with chopped herbs, oil, vinegar or lemon, and pepper and salt. They
may be used alone, or mixed with finely-chopped onion and other
salad vegetables. Puff-balls, Ceps *(Boletus edulis),* and the Common
Mushroom are among the species which are excellent in raw salads.
Cooked Salads
An even greater variety of wild mushrooms may be used for cooked
salads. The mushrooms are sliced and then simmered until tender,
either in oil or in salted water. You drain them, allow them to cool,
and then proceed as for raw salads above.

CREAMED WILD MUSHROOMS
Remove stalks. Unless caps are quite small slice into $\frac{1}{4}''$ slices. Sweat
these gently in butter over a low heat with a little chopped onion or
crushed garlic. Add pepper and salt and chopped parsley and, when
the mushrooms are tender, enough cream just to cover them.
Continue to cook, while stirring gently, until cream thickens. Serve
on hot toast.

This is equally good as a breakfast dish (in which case the onion or
garlic may be omitted) or served as a Savoury at other meals.

WILD MUSHROOMS PROVENÇALE
Cut off stems. Soak mushrooms for an hour in olive oil. Heat some
oil in a frying pan. Take the mushrooms out of the cold oil, drain,
sprinkle with pepper, salt, chopped onion, a little finely-chopped
garlic, and chopped parsley and fry for about 5 minutes over a brisk
heat.

WILD MUSHROOMS and TOMATOES

1 lb. Mushrooms	2 ozs. chopped Bacon
1 lb. Tomatoes	1½ ozs. Butter or cooking-fat
2 Onions (sliced)	Seasoning

Dip the tomatoes in boiling water, remove skins, and slice. Fry the
chopped bacon in the fat, then add the sliced onion and cook until
golden. Now add the mushrooms (sliced), the tomatoes, and pepper
and salt, and simmer gently for about 30 minutes with the lid on.
Finally, sprinkle a little flour over the mixture and cook gently while
stirring until the sauce thickens.

MORELS WITH CREAM

Morels should be gathered only in dry weather. They should be picked as clean as possible and then well-rinsed and washed in running water. Dry thoroughly, cut off the lower part of the stem, and then split longtitudinally. Stew them for about 30 minutes with butter, a little stock, chopped parsley and any other chopped herbs, and pepper and salt. Finally bind with a whipped egg-yolk and a little cream and serve on fried bread.

STUFFED MORELS

Cut off the lower part of the stem and clean as above, but do not split the Morels. After cleaning they are filled with a stuffing of chopped bacon, bread-crumbs, chopped onion and parsley, and dripping. Wrap round with a thin bacon rasher and tie. The morels are then gently-simmered in stock for about 30 minutes, and served on toast.

Finally, since Tuffles are also fungi, here is a mid-Victorian recipe for cooking one, in case any reader is ever lucky enough to find or acquire one!

MUSHROOM COD

(This recipe, reprinted by courtesy of the Fish Information Service, uses button mushrooms. Though as yet untested by the writer, it should certainly apply equally to any of the delicate, capped, wild varieties–especially when young.)

1 lb. Cod Fillet	Salt and Pepper
4 ozs. Button Mushrooms	chopped Parsley
1 small Onion	Milk
2 ozs. Butter	aluminium foil 18 in. by 18 in.
1 ozs. plain Flour	

Skin the fish and cut into three even-sized pieces. Wash and dry. Season the fish with salt and pepper and toss in flour. Put the aluminium foil on to a baking-tin and grease the centre area with a little melted butter. Place the cod pieces in the centre. Wash and slice the mushrooms. Peel and chop the onion.

Heat 1 oz. butter in a saucepan and cook the mushrooms and onion gently until softened, but not brown. Spoon on to the fish. (Reserve any butter in the pan for a sauce.)

Fold the sides of the foil and overlap the edges, forming a loose parcel. Bake at 375°F., Gas No. 5, for 35-40 minutes. Open the foil and drain the juices into a measuring-jug. Make the juices up to ½ pint with milk. Cook for 1 minute. Add the liquid, stirring all the time, and bring to the boil. Season to taste. Pour the sauce over the fish and sprinkle with chopped parsley.

Tested recipe   Serves 3

The above are fairly conventional mushroom recipes. The

following are for gourmets. (Since those who try them are unlikely to need specified quantities, these are left to individual tastes.) Good cooking is much easier than most people imagine, and it is sometimes great fun, and no more expensive than an evening at the local to try out some of the following 'Finer Fare'.)

TRUFFLES* A LA PERIGORD
The truffle is prepared simply by rinsing in cold water, gently scrubbing with a brush if necessary, and drying in a cloth. Then put into a stew-pan some slices of bacon, and lay the truffles on them. Sprinkle with salt and a leaf or two of bay. Cover all with champagne. Close the pan tightly, and boil half an hour. Serve the truffles alone, on a napkin.

The above recipe is included on the assumption that anyone who can afford truffles (at about 30/- each) can also, presumably, afford to boil a bottle of champagne and then throw the wine away!

There is now quite unexpected news that will happily perhaps soon make the above assumption unnecessary (at least in respect of the price of truffles).

The Times Saturday Review, May 25th, 1968, prints an article by Peter Nichols under the heading 'A Truffle Trove in the Desert'. It begins: 'If anything looked certain to the gourmet and the economist alike it was that no one in their right minds would look for truffles in a desert. But the unthinkable has happened and Botswana, the former Bechuanaland, may well be destined to see its economy enriched, by the discovery of a supply of truffles in the Kalahari desert.'

The article describes how an U.N.F.A.O. official tested their culinary properties last February by serving them whole, like roast potatoes, with a joint. Last May 7th, Mr. and Mrs. Vernon Jarrett tested them at their famous *George's*, Rome's leading international

---

* Truffles do indeed grow in Britain, mainly 3–4″ underground, in Beech-woods, from October to February. Because they grow underground Truffles have to be hunted with the help of pigs or hounds whose sense of smell has been trained to detect them. (The best account of Truffles will be found in Dr. John Ramsbottom's book, *Mushrooms and Toadstools,* detailed in the Bibliography.)

The English species is *Tuber aestivum* and, though sufficiently good to have kept professional truffle-hunters presumably gainfully occupied for some 250 years ending in 1939, is not considered by gourmets comparable with the French Périgord Truffle, *Tuber melanosporum,* or with the Italian Truffle from Piedmont, the *Tuber magnatum.* For a noted gourmet's appreciation of the White Trufflles of Northern Italy see pp. 43–44 of *Italian Food* by Elizabeth David, Penguin Books. I regret to place on record that, early this 1967, superb black Truffles from Périgord with a superb aroma, were priced in London at 30/- each!

restaurant, and 'Everybody was delighted with what was served'.

This article is worth study by all lovers of wild mushrooms, not only for the interest of this new discovery, but also for Mr. Jarrett's quoted classical hints for a fine cèpes recipe, *Sauce Mornay, sou cloche,* for 'cotes de Veau Tallerand' garnished with *cannoliche,* and for his mouth-watering *Chapon truffé.*

CODDLED MUSHROOMS WITH CODDLED EGG

(Per person) 1 Egg	2 Teaspoons Cream
1 Teaspoon Butter	1 average sized
2 Teaspoons chopped	Wild Mushroom cap
fresh Herbs	Seasoning

Coddle egg (usual method: 5 minutes in boiling-hot water off fire). Coddle whole mushroom cap with egg in same water (slightly salted) but only for 2½ minutes. Remove cap, slice. Tip half sliced mushrooms into warm cup. Chop herbs roughly. Egg now ready. Crack smartly on cup edge into two halves. Yolk (unbroken) and most of creamy white fall into cup. Scoop into cup remainder of coddled white. Add butter, remainder of sliced mushroom, cream and herbs. Season. (Tested, O.G.)   Time 6 minutes

WILD MUSHROOMS WITH ALLIOLI (improved)

Put an egg yolk, chopped garlic to taste, one teaspoon wet bread-crumbs, salt, fresh-ground black pepper, a little (say ½ teaspoon) thin-sliced spring onion or chopped chives, mustard and a few drops of wine vinegar into a mortar. Pound.

Then add oil as though making mayonnaise, and proceed as for mayonnaise.

When the consistency of ointment, sharpen, if desired, with a few drops of lemon juice and garnish with chopped fresh herbs.

(Tested, O.G.)

Allioli is a Mallorcan speciality: a flavoured, bread-thickened mayonnaise. It can be heightened, like mayonnaise, with such additions as here suggested. It blends well with mushrooms and helps all the duller edible varieties, either chilled in the refrigerator and added to hot grilled, or fried, caps or added to raw, sliced caps, served as a salad.

CLEAR BEETROOT and WILD MUSHROOM SOUP
(CZERWONY BARSZCZ z USZKAMI)

(This dish is included in the traditional Polish supper *(Wigilia)* on Christmas Eve)

First make clear beetroot stock. Peel raw beetroots, cut into ½ inch cubes and simmer, with a few bay leaves and peppercorns, in slightly salted water until the water is deep red.

Pour off and keep the claret-coloured stock.

Repeat with the *same* cubes of beetroot, using fresh water each time, until the beetroot no longer colours the boiling water red.

(The beetroot is discarded. The stock will keep for about three days).

Take dried cêpes and soak in water until soft. Remove, drain and dry. Fry chopped onion in butter until brown. Add the cêpes sliced, seasoning (if liked, also a little paprika) and fry on low fire for a few minutes. Allow to cool.

Prepare (water and seasoned flour) small, (ravioli-sized) flour-paste cases.

Mince finely the cooled, mushroom-onion mixture and insert—as though for ravioli—into cases. Seal as for ravioli.

Bake the cases in medium oven until golden-brown (without added fat).

Heat the beetroot stock, sharpen (to taste) with either vinegar or fresh lemon juice and put into warmed soup plates. At the last moment add an appropriate quantity of the hot, golden-brown cases and serve.

This dish, received from a lady of Polish origin, is included for its obvious charm. The same or a very similar, dish has been published by the great French culinary author, Édouard de Pomiane.

(Quantities are not given, since those sufficiently interested in elegant cuisine to take the trouble to prepare this soup will clearly not need them.)

CHINESE MUSHROOMS
Several varieties, dried or canned (and, therefore, not to be compared in flavour with the fresh ones, but nevertheless always interesting), can be bought in Chinese provision stores in larger cities. They can also be sampled in Chinese restaurants.

It adds interest to a Chinese dinner, or many other kinds, prepared at home, to make a dish of Chinese mushrooms.

If the dried varieties are used they should first be soaked for an hour or two in a little cold water. Take them out, drain them and save the water. Slice them fairly coarsely and fry in medium-hot lard for a matter of seconds to 1 minute, together with sliced spring onions and/or sliced celery, and/or very coarsely chopped watercress; and/or some fresh bean sprouts.

Add a few drops of soya sauce and a very small quantity of medium dry sherry and season to taste. Fry another 30 seconds. The sauce can be thickened with cornflour.

An equally good and perhaps more interesting dish—an imitation of Chinese mushrooms—can be made by preparing selected fresh wild capped varieties in this way.

WILD MUSHROOMS and JACKET POTATOES (A simple, late-night supper dish)

Put the scrubbed floury potatoes into a low oven *before* you go to the theatre.

Around midnight, sauté selected wild mushrooms in butter. Season.

Take the potatoes out of the oven and cross-quarter. Open out. Heap the cooked mushrooms into the opening. Check for salt.

Pour over the mushroom-flavoured melted butter.

(The following recipes, gratefully received from an Irish lady, are included as they appear to evoke a pronounced and genuine 'mushroom' flavour even from the normally less-flavoured cultivated species.)

IRISH MUSHROOM SAUCE

Break clean, *unpeeled* caps and stems of raw mushrooms into lumps and pulp in a blender. Season; warm with a little butter and serve. (This sauce is especially good with buttered *vermicelli*.)

IRISH MUSHROOM SOUP

Add milk to the above sauce. Heat to near boiling. Serve.

The writer tested these simple recipes with ordinary cultivated mushrooms bought from a greengrocer and was delighted to find the flavour nearly equal to that of fresh-picked field mushrooms!

The recipes were also tested by fine-mincing the raw mushrooms instead of using a blender. Flavour was equally excellent. The soup had a coarser texture, more like a good 'peasant soup'.

There are obvious promising possibilities, using the various wild species in place of cultivated mushrooms.

INDEX